ABUELA, DON'T FORGET ME

ABUELA, DON'T FORGET ME

REX OGLE

NORTON YOUNG READERS

An Imprint of W. W. Norton & Company
Independent Publishers Since 1923

To Catalina,
my very own angel.
I will love you forever.

For information about permission to reproduce selections from this book, write to Permissions, W. W. Norton & Company, Inc., 500 Fifth Avenue, New York, NY 10110

For information about special discounts for bulk purchases, please contact W. W. Norton Special Sales at specialsales@wwnorton.com or 800-233-4830

Manufacturing by Lake Book Manufacturing
Book design by Hana Anouk Nakamura
Production manager: Beth Steidle

ISBN 978-1-324-01995-4

W. W. Norton & Company, Inc., 500 Fifth Avenue, New York, N.Y. 10110
www.wwnorton.com

W. W. Norton & Company Ltd., 15 Carlisle Street, London W1D 3BS

0 9 8 7 6 5 4 3 2 1

CONTENTS

Foreword

These days, when I call my abuela, the conversation goes in circles. She says, *"How are you? How's work? I'm so glad you graduated from college, education is so important. How are you? How's work? I'm so glad you graduated from college, education is so important. How are you? How's work? I'm so glad you graduated from college. . . ."* When I try to break the loop or introduce a new topic, it doesn't go well. Abuela becomes confused. *"Excuse me? Sir? What time is it? I have to go."* My abuela is having a hard time remembering things because she—the most important person in my life—is living with dementia.

My abuela is the woman who encouraged me to read and write at an early age. Who bought groceries when my mom was unemployed and we were living on food stamps. She is the woman who offered her home to me when the violence at my mom's became too much. Abuela is the woman who got me off the streets after my father kicked me out for being gay. She told me if I wanted to be a novelist, then I should pursue it, that if I worked hard, I could accomplish anything. By every definition of the word, my grandmother is an angel. My own personal fairy godmother. Abuela is the only parent I've ever known who showed me truly unconditional love, kindness, and support.

And now she is forgetting me.

Most days, she knows who I am. But sometimes, she struggles. She forgets that I left my job to write full-time. She forgets that I have two brothers. She forgets that I am married, that she was at my wedding in the front row in the first seat. And sometimes . . . sometimes she gets a little confused about who I am. Though she seems unfazed, her lack of recall is devastating for me.

But I don't let her know that. I answer each and every

question as if she were asking it for the first time. I talk slowly and with a buoyed heart, that I might bring some joy into her day. I try to show her the same love and compassion she showed me through all those years of my innocent childhood, my depressed (and angry) teenage years, and my anxiety-riddled college years. I can be strong for her, because she was always strong for me . . . though when I get off the phone, or leave her house, I cry long and hard, feeling like a forgotten child.

So I write. I sit down, write a few lines about my abuela, and revel in it, cherishing a recollection captured on a single page, losing myself in the echoes of the past. Reading them again, it's like wrapping myself in an electric blanket (like the one Abuela put on my bed). As if I were back in Abuela's guest room, scratch-scratch-scratching at my chicken pox, while she feeds me chicken soup with noodles. Or holding her soft brown hand in a library, as we pick out books. Or picking pecans in her backyard, as she tells me about growing up in Mexico with nothing to eat. Or her carrying me to safety, a swarm of angry geese chasing after us for running out of stale bread crusts to toss them.

Most of the poems I share with her. A few have left her confused about what it is she's reading. But others? They make her clap her hands, and say, "I remember that pecan tree. I remember those horrible geese. You are such a good writer. Will you share more with me?"

She may forget. And one day, I may forget too. But for now, the memories are captured, like insects in amber, ready to survive for millions of years. My memories of a wonderful woman are written in words and verses and fragments in this book, unable to be *un*written.

And if it is forgotten, it can always be read again.

1
ABUELA'S HOUSE

hamper

The end of her hallway has
four doors for people, and
two much-smaller doors for elves,
opening into an empty space
the size of a laundry basket
or a little boy.
Built into the wall,
the wooden doors, smooth and lush brown,
like a Kit Kat milk chocolate bar,
or Abuela's skin, silky and soft.

I am four-years-young
and still learning to speak up,
so ask, *"What's in there?"*
Abuela, her lips curled at the corners, proud that I am hungry
    to know,
answers, "For ropa sucia, dirty laundry. A hamper."
I laugh, rolling the new word in my mouth, like a gumball,
"Hamper? Hamper. Hamper!"
It feels the same on my tongue as *hamburger* and so
I squeal, *"Hamper-ger!"*

At times when no one sees me,
all eyes on my mom, shouting, ranting, screaming (again),
accusing others of this and of that,
I run away,
scamper to the hamper, like a mouse.
Opening the bottom door, climbing inside
into the darkness,
slowing my breathing, inhaling drywall and fabric softener,
hiding,
waiting for someone to remember (and seek)
me.

My giggles cannot be stopped,
they rush out like ants from a kicked mound, but
more joyous, like birds racing toward the sun.
Even if I bite my fingers to stop them,
the silly escapes,
"*Hee-hee-hee-hee-hee-hee-hee-hee*,"
refusing to be held back until

the top door of the hamper lifts,
Abuela's face appears, warm
haloed by the hall light,
a heavenly angel to scare away the shadows,
asking, "Hola, hamper. Have you seen mi nieto, my
    grandson?"

This makes me laugh so hard,
I tumble out
onto her brown feet, sheathed in pastel blue cotton slippers,
as I squeal, like a delighted piglet,
"*¡Estoy aquí! I'm your grandson!*"

te amo siempre

When Abuela sees me, she tells me,
"Te amo. Te amo siempre."
"What's that mean?"
"It means, I love you. I love you forever."
So I try to say it, *"Tea ammo sim-pray."*
I slap my own face. *"I did it wrong. I'm so dumb."*
"Do not hit yourself. You were very close. Try again."
Then she repeats, slower for me, "Tay ya-mo."
"Te amo."
"Te amo siempre."
"Te amo siempre. What's it mean again?"
"I love you. And I will love you forever."
"And I will," she says, "forever."

And she will.
No matter how many times I mess up.

ear—kiss—POP!

My mom refuses to live in the same town as her mom.
But when we visit Abilene,
or Abuela visits us,
the first thing my grandmother does
is embrace me,
her cheeks soft with powder, a silk kerchief tied round her neck,
and pulls my ear to her lips,
whispering, "Tu eres mi futuro,"
then, *MWAH*!!
sucking the air out with a kiss, making my ear hole *POP*!

I push her away,
squealing, giggling,
"Don't kiss on my ear!"

She laughs.
Then kisses the other ear
                              the exact
                                         same
                                              way.

1214 South Jackson Drive

"I am lucky to have my own home," Abuela tells me.
"In Mexico, we had nothing. One room, dirt floors, no running
    water.
A small shack for mi familia: my parents, my brothers and
    sisters, and me. But now . . ."

Now, her home is
red bricks, white trim, white wood beams, a white tin roof.

Three bedrooms. Two bathrooms.
Living room. Two-car garage.
Back and front yards.
Yellow grass in the winter, yellow grass in the summer
because green does not last
in the Texas hill country heat.

White walls in the halls, and bedrooms,
the living room paneled by wood (that isn't real wood)
and a stone fireplace, with wood beams (that *is* real wood).
Throughout the house
the carpet, dark and deep red, scratchy
maroon, like a scabbed knee two days after falling.
Bathrooms and kitchen are laid with tan linoleum (that looks
    like tiles, but isn't).
The kitchen is bright, like my Crayola crayon, "Dandelion."
Yellow fridge, yellow oven, yellow stove
yellow and white checkered tablecloth, like a picnic basket
    blanket.
Though the countertops are the same color as
the tree leaves outside,
green, like the dreams of the envious grass below
wishing it wasn't so thirsty
under the Texas sun.

from

Abuela rocks me in her arms
even as I squirm
like a worm.
"Do you know where you were born, mijo?"
"In the ocean! Agua! With clown fish!"
Her eyes, her smile, light up like the sun
as she shakes her head, "No. You were born here, in Abilene,
    Texas, at Dyess Air Force Base,
where your daddy was a soldier. Your mom is my daughter."
"Nuh-uh! I was born in the sky, from black birds, and I flew with them
to the moon and back! We drank the stars like leche!"
"Your mom was young when she had you. Only twenty. She
    wanted you more than she wanted college, which was free,
    because her father, my husband, died for his country.
She was so beautiful then. Hair down to her waist.
She is beautiful still. Though her hair is shorter.
After you, she never went back to school."
When Abuela speaks of my mom . . .
Her eyes, her smile, dim dark like caves at night,
her lips tighten into a thin line, forcing her mouth to say nice
    things
by speaking only facts.

But I am too young to know facts from fiction.
"My mom is a crow, my father is a mouse!
He only eats queso! And corn chips!"
Abuela rocks me in her arms again
trying to kiss my ear
as I squeal and wiggle
out of her arms
and run away
arms flapping toward the sky
trying to take flight.

mijo

Leaning over, around me,
Abuela is a parachute of gentle, soft smells and softer hands,
pressing her lips to my ear, saying,
"I love you, mijo."
"What's a mee-ho?!"
"It means, son."
"I'm not the sun!"
"You are my first grandson, my daughter's son. So you are my
    son too."
"Say that then. Why say me-ho?"
Sun breaks in through the window, lighting her eyes,
brilliant brown, with flecks of green, like underwater in a
    swimming hole.
"Mijo is what my mamá called mis hermanos, my brothers,
so I say it to you,
not in English,
but my first language, Español."
"What is my language?"

"You speak English," Mom interrupts, her tone hard like an old
    hammer,
"and you are *my* son. *Not* hers."

When my mom looks at her mom, eyebrows pointed in and
    down, furrowed and narrow,
Abuela bows her head to look at the floor,
and says nothing else.

names

With delicate precision,
Abuela writes my name on lined paper,
REX EARL OGLE III.
She hands me her pencil.
"Do you want to try?"
Snorting and giggling,
I write, CAT.
Abuela says, "That is not your name, silly grandson. Your
    name is Rex."
"Your name is 'Buela."
"That is what you call me. Me llamo es Catalina Caldwell.
Before I was married, I was Catalina Ignacia Benevides."
"I can spell that!" I say.
I write CAT again,
my giggle growing to laughter.

Abuela adds more letters, so that CAT becomes CATALINA.
Before my eyes, Abuela shows me
                         how letters
                             make words
                                  like magic.

chicken spaghetti

"Wha'cha making?!"

Abuela answers, "Chicken spaghetti."

I shake my head, *"No!*

Silly 'Buela! Chicken doesn't go in spaghetti!

Meatballs go in spaghetti. Meat! Chicken goes in chicken."

"You can put chicken in different things. I like to put shredded
    chicken with pasta.

The recipe is from Reader's Digest."

"I don't want chicken spaghetti.

I want tacos. Crunchy tacos with cheese. No lettuce or tomato."

"Tomorrow. Tonight, we will have chicken spaghetti."

"No! I don't want it."

"Have you ever tried it?"

I shake my head, *"No."*

"Perhaps you should try it then."

"It looks weird."

"When I was a little girl, my family often went hungry.

We were lucky if each of us had one tortilla, with a little bit of
    arroz y frijoles, rice and beans.

You are lucky that I can offer you so much. Will you try it? For
    me?"

"One bite . . . for you . . . but I won't like it."

Her fork dips into the crockpot, returning with noodles, shreds
of white breast meat, dressed in red sauce, steaming with heat.

Abuela blows, so my tongue will not be scalded.

In my mouth, it is creamy, with a hint of pepper and sweetness,
a touch of Abuela's home, a spice called cumin.

My eyes grow wide,

"Delicious! Can I have more?"

"Nah. You said you did not want any. I think I will keep it all
    for me."

*"'Buela! Please, just a little bowl? It's my favorite in the whole wide
    world!"*

I whine, and beg for what I did not want a moment before.
Her smile lets me in on her gentle trick.
"You can have as much as you want.
You will not go hungry—not while I live."

por favor y gracias

"*I need this,*" I say, then louder,
"*I NEED THIS!*"
My little hands, shaking, holding
a small pink bear, a pleasant rainbow etched in red-yellow-
    green-blue on his white tummy.
"*This is Cheer Bear, I need him so bad.*"
I hug the plastic package, desperate to rip it open, free my
    cartoon friend, and take him home.
"*'Buela! Did you hear me?*"
She raises a finger to her lips.
"Shhh. We do not yell in stores. We do not make a scene."
Like my mother, I think.
Abuela extends her hand to me.
Reluctantly, I give up the toy for her to see, adding, "*He's my
    friend.*"
She studies the bear, then studies me.
"Your friend is not a boy, she is a girl."
"*No, that's a mistake. He's a boy, like me. I need him.*"
"But he is pink."
"*Pink is good! Like strawberry cake, my favorite!*"
She hesitates,
though I don't know why
it is wrong for a boy to play with a pink toy.

But my joy
      is her world,
           evident in my fingers, as they reach up   for love.

Abuela takes my right hand and kisses it.
"Mijo, *need* is different from *want*.
You *need* clean water and food and a roof.
A toy, you only *want*."
"*Then I want him!*"

"Then what do you say?"
Confused, I speak,
"I want Cheer Bear?"
"You must say por favor. Please."
"Poor flavor. And pleeeeeeeeeeeease!"
She places the toy in her shopping basket.
"And now you say . . . ?"
"I love you!"
She cannot hide her grin, though she tries to be stern,
"You say gracias. Thank you."
"But I do love you."
"This I know. But love is not gratitude.
You must be polite. Always say por favor y gracias. To
    everyone.
Even a cashier or janitor. Everyone deserves respect."
I do not leave Abuela's side in the air force base commissary,
eyes glued to my new friend,
trapped within plastic, imprisoned in a basket,
that I cannot have until he is paid for.

At the cash register, I shiver with desire
so eager to hold the Care Bear, as the cashier rings up
a toothbrush *BEEP!*
a notepad *BEEP!*
a lotion *BEEP!*
before finally moving Cheer Bear from conveyor belt to
    scanner *BEEP!*
Before he is lost in the brown plastic bag,
I grab him and hug him and squeal, *"POR FAVOR Y
    GRACIAS!"*

After she has paid, Abuela walks me outside,
opening her gift to her grandson, a pink bear,
so I can be the truest version
of me.

ducks

On the counter
lies half a loaf of bread
in its plastic bag
"Baked Fresh" by Mrs. Baird's.
(I do not know Mrs. Baird, but she might be a friend of
    Abuela's from church.)

I steal a piece, putting it in my mouth,
expecting the white to be fluffy and soft like air. Instead, I spit
    it out,
"This bread is hard!"
"It is stale," Abuela says, "I was saving it for the ducks."
"Ducks eat bread?"
"Si, señor."
"See what?"
"No. Si. It is Spanish for yes."
"What is no?"
"No."

Under the afternoon sun,
we stroll from the parking lot
to the pond, where the ducks wait,
hunger in their eyes, like Wile E. Coyote
as he waits for the Road Runner.
When I throw a whole slice, they attack it.
Abuela shakes her head.
"It will last longer, if you start small."
She shows me how to tear the bread into small pieces,
and throw, one at a time
rather than all at once.

The ducks quack.
I quack back, *"Quack-Quack, don't look at my crack!"*

and wiggle my butt at them.
Abuela says, "Do not be lewd."
She tries to hide her grin
when I do it again.

We enjoy feeding the ducks
until the geese come
honking
and hissing
aggressive
surrounding us as I throw them bread,
but one piece at a time is not enough for all of them.
One bites my hand and I scream shrilly.
As another lunges at me,
Abuela picks me up over her head,
kicks away the vicious bird,
and runs for the car
rescuing me
from the angry mob of feathers and bills and flapping wings
    that follow
wanting to devour
my tiny fingers.

Before this, I did not know Abuela was tough or strong,
like a superhero from a comic or cartoon,
like Spiderman or Batman.

She is a hero.

Now, I know.

library

Pulling up to the large public building,
Abuela glows with pride.
"This is the public library."
"I know it's a li-berry."
"LibRary," she corrects me,
her voice, soft as a bluebonnet petal.

Inside, white walls reach toward blue skies
seen through high glass windows
resting above shelf after shelf after shelf of
book after book after book.
My eyes grow wide, whites wider, pupils dilating,
to take in all these stories
begging to be known.

"Can I read them all?" I ask.
Abuela smiles.
"Yes.
If you work hard, you can do anything."

prayer

I am a dinosaur
devouring my prey
when dinner is placed before me.

"Before we eat, we pray,"
Abuela says.
"Why?"
"To let God know we are thankful."
"But you are the one who bought the food. Who made it."
"But God is the one who provided it."
I do not understand.

"Mom doesn't pray,"
I say, biting another chicken nugget.

Abuela says,
"I am not your mom."

pecans

In the fall,
Abuela's backyard trees are so full
the branches drop low, starting to let go
pod after pod after pod
of pecans
until the yard is littered, with round shells of
brown and tan and black,
like a squirrel's coat.

"What are those? Tree eggs?"
"They are nuts," Abuela answers.
I say, *"Nuts don't grow on trees!"*
She says, "Pecans do."
"No! Nuts come from the store."
"Where do you think nuts from the store come from? They are
    not grown in jars.
They grow on trees first.
These are better. They are fresh."
Abuela shakes the tree. The pods fall like rain.
falling on one another, *clack-clack-clack*.
I dance under, hands raised, trying to catch them in hand,
as I would with fireflies.

With a rake, Abuela gathers them into piles.
"Why do you eat something from a tree?"
"The best food comes from trees:
Bananas, oranges, apples."
"I only like sour green apples! Red apples are gross."
Abuela says, "You should not be so picky.
In Mexico, we had little food for my brothers and sisters, and
    Mamá y Papá.
Now, I have food that grows in my very own yard.
I am grateful . . .

For my trees. For my job. For this country.
For you."

I leap into the air, holding the branch like a monkey,
pulling and shaking,
so more pods rain down, on me, then onto the ground with the
    others,
clack-clack-clack-clack-clack-clack.
I ask, *"Can we eat them now?"*
"We need to let them dry.
In two weeks, they will be perfect."
"Two weeks?! That's too long! I won't be here."
"Las cosas buenas vienan a aquellos que esperan."
"Huh?"
"Good things come to those who wait."

In two weeks,
Abuela will spend her free time
cracking shells
dislodging nuts from their wombs
sealing them in Ziploc bags,
dating them with a black permanent marker
before storing the pecans in her freezer or lining her pantry shelves
top to bottom
like books in a library.
She will have so many nuts,
she will have to give them away.

I will have left Abilene by then,
returned home to my mother.
But a cardboard box will arrive in the mail
addressed only to me.
Inside, I will find
clear bags packed full to the red-and-blue-makes-purple seal
with freshly shelled pecans.

In my mouth, the sweet nutty crunch
releases oil as I chew and chew and chew
until the pecans melt on my tongue
like butter.

2
TO AND FROM

shoes

"My husband died in Vietnam, so that we could have these
 benefits," Abuela says.
"At the Air Force Base commissary, we do not have to pay tax."
"Rex doesn't need them!" Mom snaps, like the turtle that once
 bit my finger.
"But I want them! Por favor y gracias!"
"Don't speak Spanish like you know how! You don't! And you
 don't need shoes!"
People look toward my mom's voice, loud and
raised, like the hair on an angry cat's back.
Abuela does not point at my shoes, too small for my feet,
 covered in dirt, eaten by holes.
Instead, she says, "Let me buy them for him . . .
for his birthday, for his first day of first grade. He is growing so
 fast."

Mom throws her hands up,
shouting, "Fine! Do whatever you want. You always do
 anyway!"
People watch because people always watch,
when Mom shouts in public.

Abuela's smile is not a smile.
It is thin,
pressed together,
like two slices of white bread, smashed,
with no meat or cheese or mayonnaise or mustard between
 them.
Just smooshed-down bread, crushed.

Abuela leans in, whispering in my ear,
"You will look nice on your first day of school . . .
even if tu madre me mata . . ."

lemonade

When we arrive at 1214 South Jackson Drive, unannounced, it
    is late
under cover of night. Mom slams her palm against the door,
BANG BANG BANG
presses the doorbell
DING DING DING DING
tears streaking down her face
The porch light comes on, Abuela appears in a housecoat,
    worry in her eyes.
She ushers us inside,
makes light from lamps in the living room,
warning shadows away by embracing me. I yawn while Mom
    cries and shouts.

Mom is always crying and shouting
ever since the thick orange envelope arrived from my dad's
    lawyers.
In the living room, I spin myself around spinning spinning
    spinning
hyper from the candy I ate in the dark of the car drive
until Mom screams at me, "Stop it, Rex!!"
I fall down dizzy onto my Star Wars pillow and ask Abuela,
    "Can I have some lemonade?"
Abuela says, "It is late. Tomorrow, you will have all the
    lemonade you want."
She escorts me past the hamper, into my room, tucks me in
    bed, and kisses my forehead
once, then again, and again,
saying, "Good night, and sweet dreams, mijo."

Even with the door closed, I hear Mom,
her shouting-crying a familiar lullaby,
as I close my eyes, thinking of Abuela, who knows that I know
    that she always remembers

to have lemonade, made just for me, in her fridge
waiting ice-cold in her mustard-yellow Tupperware pitcher,
the one with the suction button that you have to press on top.
I know she did not forget, she just didn't know we were coming.
I am not mad, like my mom.
I know Abuela, and the lemonade, will be there in the
    morning,
whether my mom is here, or not.

pencils

At the Dyess Air Force Base commissary,
I follow Mom and Abuela.
They whisper in the aisle,
while I look at colored pencils.
Abuela squeezes Mom's hand, saying,
"You will get through this."
"Get through what?"
"The divorce," Mom snaps at me.
"What's a divorce?"
"Your dad left. And he's not coming back."
"He's left before. He always comes back."
Mom shouts at me, "Not this time!"

I think of my dad, whose name I share, whose nose I share,
who likes old westerns like I do, likes black-and-white monster
    movies like I do,
who buys me Star Wars figures, and cuts the crusts from my
    sandwiches . . .
I think of my dad and never seeing him again
and a pit opens inside me
that swallows everything
and then I am crying
and Mom is shouting at me to stop it,
even as Abuela hugs me
and tells Mom to let me be
to let me cry
and Mom says,
"He's always crying.
That's another reason his dad left."
and walks away.

neighbor

The morning after a day of crying,
I wake.
Abuela kisses both my ears
POP! POP!
and feeds me microwaved chicken-spaghetti and lemonade.
When I am done, I ask,
"Can I play with Jason?"
Mom says,
"No! You're here to visit your grandmother."
Though Abuela tells me,
"It is okay. Go. Play. Have fun. I am not going anywhere."

I stick my tongue out at Mom,
and run out the front door,
not caring about the shouting
I have started
and
     left
         far
              behind.

                    Because I know . . .
            it will be waiting for me when I return.
                      It always is.

backyard

Jason's house is across South Jackson Drive from Abuela's.
It is one story,
painted yellow like sunshine,
with a blue truck parked in the yard, because the other two
    spots are taken.

I ring the doorbell.
Jason's mom answers the door, hair in curlers, a cigarette
    between her fingers.
"Is Jason here? Can he play?"
Behind his mother's skirt, he appears
sandy hair and green eyes, a smile
with teeth crooked like mine.
He waves me inside,
their walls with the same fake wood panels as Abuela's,
though her house is cleaner.
We do not stay inside,
under the vent blowing machine cold.
Jason slides open the glass door
and the screen door
to reveal a wonderland under the bright Texas sun.

Jason's backyard has
a red metal swing set with a blue plastic slide
a yellow wooden sandbox holding a small beach of sand
a giant tree, a small treehouse leaning against its trunk
an orange cabinet with water guns and footballs and action
    figures of G.I. Joe, Star Wars, and a few Barbies his older
    sister left to die
at our hands, in our wars, with boy action figures
because boys can't play with dolls unless we are destroying
    them.

We are children
so the world is still beautiful
and war
            still only a game.

first day

The phone cries *RING*!
and I run to answer it *RING*!
dragging a chair from the table *RING*!
to the wall, climbing onto the chair, reaching for the *RING*!
"Hello?!"
"Is this my favorite grandson in the whole wide world?"
"I'm your only grandson."
"No. You have a cousin," Abuela reminds me.
"I was first. Donald doesn't count."
She laughs. "How was your first week of school, mijo?"
"Stupid."
"Do not use that word. You are smarter than that."
"Am not. I'm dumb. Alice said so. At recess, Jimmy said my name is a
dog's name. And Shannon said I'm poor 'cause I only have six crayons,
and the red one is broke."
"Do not listen to them. They are wrong. You are smart. I will
buy you more crayons.
And you have a good name. Muy fuerte."
"What's fuerte mean?"
"Strong."
"I'm not strong. Playing music chairs I fell, and lost the game on the first
try.
It's not fair, I didn't know how."
"You will do better next time."
"The lunch lady made me eat peas. I almost threw up!"
Abuela asks,
"Did anything happen this week that you did like?"
"Um . . ." I say, waiting, thinking . . .
"Talking to you."
"Same, mijo. Same."

books on tape

The next time I go to Abilene, to Abuela's,
there is a cassette player waiting in my room
with a shiny gold sticker: Property of Abilene Public Library.
"Did you steal this from the library?"
I say to Abuela, in shock.
She laughs.
"No, I asked permission. You can borrow anything from the
    library."
"Why did you borrow it?"
"For you. For books on tape."
I thought tapes were only for music,
and am pleasantly surprised to learn otherwise.
Abuela drives me to the public library,
leading me by hand, mine in hers, through the aisles,
to shelves full of plastic cases
containing cassette tapes and books
so you can follow the words while listening to the "Read
    Aloud."
I do not understand that someone else, somewhere else, made
    these.
Instead I believe
Abuela made these
                for me
because she knows how much
                I love stories.

boo!

I slide the white tape into the black cassette player
and press PLAY.
The book in my hands comes to life,
haunted music in the air,
and the ghost saying, "ooooooooooooh . . ."

Four pages in,
I am too scared to continue.

I run out of the room
to Abuela
and cry
"There's a monster in the book in my room!"

She carries the book
and the tape
and puts them both in the freezer
so that I can sleep tonight,
safe from ghosts.

under the stars

1214 South Jackson Drive
smells the same
as it always does
(like lemon, pine cleaner, and fresh powder)

sounds the same
as it always does
(quiet, except crickets outside and the air conditioner inside)

looks the same
as it always does
(clean and sparse, Abuela giving away everything she does not need)

tastes the same
as it always does
(sweet tart lemonade, never enough sugar)

feels the same
as it always does
(scratchy red carpet under foot, and too cold, giving goosebumps in
    spite of summer).

Abuela likes things to stay the same.
Always.
. . . except . . .
in my room
when I turn out the lights
I discover the ceiling has been decorated with new constellations
    that glow in the dark
as if Abuela has stolen from the sky,
from the heavens and angels and god himself
to make a gift
            of stars
                    just for me.

stripes

The summer sun heats the Texas earth,
bricks and metal and concrete heated so hot
until you cannot touch them, or walk barefoot
around the public pool
without scorching the
sole of your foot.

From the changing room,
I run to the aquatic sway of clear blue.
the lifeguard's whistle *blows TWEEEEEEE*,
warning me, shouts following: "No running!"
I slow, sit, then slip off hot land into refreshing water,
letting the air world slip away, left above the reflective surface.

Abuela and Aunt Lora
watch from body-long plastic chairs,
where they slather their olive brown skin
in sunscreen or oil, put on sunglasses,
hold books and magazines,
though Abuela's eyes watch me—like I watch a firework,
waiting for any danger.

Radio songs play from speakers
over the concession stand where they
offer soda, popcorn, and candy bars that melt
all over my hands in the heat.
The lifeguard's whistle cries again and again
lost among the happy screams of children.

Splashing,
waves made by swimmers,
"Marco!" shouted by one, and "Polo!" shouted by many.
I swim alone, a visitor here, a stranger

in the town where I was born.
But the only friends I need
are the diving board and my lungs,
holding my breath
watching others swim slow, make hurricanes of bubbles by
    jumping in,
even as chlorine stings my eyes,
and of course, Abuela
who waits for me with a towel
when my fingers are pruned, and
I am ready to get out.

Abuela and Lora go into the Women's locker room
and I into the Men's
to change from wet to dry clothing.

While I stand alone,
naked,
two teenagers point at me, and laugh.
"Nice stripes, wetback."
"It's a beaner-zebra!"

Something in their tone
is sharper than the lifeguard's shrill whistle.
I do not understand why
but their words drown me,
pulling me down, into the depths, before I've had a chance to
    take a breath.
Shame so heavy,
greater than the pressure in my ears when I touch the bottom
    of the deep end,
weighted, piercing
more than the sidewalk burning my soles,
as if their words
are burning my soul.

Outside, Abuela finds me in tears,
wrapped in a towel saying again and again, "*I want to go home*"
though I won't say why.
Because I do not have the vocabulary to explain this
    experience.

                                          . . . not yet.

mirror

Naked,
seven years old,
I climb onto the guest bathroom counter
to stand and stare at myself, for a long time,
in the mirror hanging over the sink.
trying to see what others see
that makes me wrong.

My toes and feet, pale white
like my father's whole frame.
My calves and knees, pecan brown,
the tops of my thighs, the color of refried beans, baked in the
    oven.
My pelvis, hidden from the sun, porcelain white,
(like a cave salamander that has never seen day)
except a penis, a mix of hazel and pink.
From fingers up past my elbows, a dark dusky bronze,
until they stop at a distinct line where shirt sleeves begin, the
    skin lighter
like my chest and belly, milk chocolate like a Twix chocolate
    bar.
My neck and face,
coffee mixed with a drop of half-and-half, or, umber, my
    crayon name for dark brown,
like Mom, Lora, and Abuela.
Though parts of me, cheeks and shoulders, have been kissed
    scarlet by the sun today,
as if preparing eyes for the
crown of blond curls atop my head
like no one in either of my families.

This.
This is all of me

as taken in by the mirror:
a striped animal, a human zebra,
painted wrong
by god's own hand.

pox

Suzie came to second grade
itch itch itching
rosy spots polka-dotting her skin like Red Hots candies,
like the game in activity books where you connect-the-dots.
Mom says I caught it from Suzie
because now I am itch itch itching too,
and look like I swam in a swarm of mosquitoes or a bed of
    Texas fire ants
and they all took turns biting me.

Mom shouts into the phone,
"I can't deal with him right now, Mother!
. . . busy . . .
. . . work . . .
. . . the divorce . . .
Just give me a break! Come pick him up!"

Abuela arrives in her gray Toyota
with a stack of library books, two coloring books, sixty-four
    crayons
(with a crayon sharpener built into the back of the box),
and a six-count snack of peanut-butter sandwiched between
    orange crackers,
wrapped in plastic with pictures of elves on the front.

Even though I can do it myself, she puts my seatbelt on.
Even though she just drove three hours to pick me up, she
    drives three hours back to Abilene.
Her smile is the sun, and the clouds go away,
her smile is warm blankets in the winter,
her smile is cartoons anytime I want,
not just on Saturday mornings.

I start itch itch itching.

"Mijo, do not scratch."

"I can't help it."

"You can. Think on something else."

I try to.

I think of the word *strawberry*

saying it again and again and again

in my head

until I cannot remember

what a strawberry is,

even though I know how to spell it.

I know what a straw is, and what a berry is,

but not a straw-berry,

unless it is a berry shaped like a straw,

or a straw made of berries.

I think so hard

my brain hurts

and has to ask

"What's a strawberry?"

Abuela answers, "A little red fruit. It is sweet."

"Oh yeah," I say, even though I cannot picture it yet.

I shift my imagination to

think of chickens running around their coop,

covered in red dots beneath their feathers

raking with their hind legs wildly

scratch scratch scratch scratching themselves until they fall
    over.

"Did Suzie get chicken pox from a chicken?"

Abuela shakes her head.

"In Mexico, I asked Mamá the same question.

She said: Son las mismas marcas cuando un pollo te picotea.

    Peck peck peck.

That means, they are the same marks as when a chicken pecks
   at you. Peck peck peck."
I say, "*You talk funny sometimes.*"

Abuela's smile fades.
"It is not funny. It is Spanish."

at church

At church,
for some reason,
I always giggle and laugh,
when everyone bows their heads in prayer,
as if I cannot control myself, when everyone is quiet.

Abuela hushes me,
"Be respectful,"
and pinches (not too hard)
where my butt cheek meets my thigh
which only makes me
laugh
harder.

abuela says

Abuela says,
jes instead of *yes*
jou instead of *you*
yob instead of *job*
proyect instead of *project*
jounger instead of *younger*
jellow instead of *yellow*
(though jelly is always jelly).

Abuela says,
bery instead of *very*
neber instead of *never*
foreber instead of *forever*
and
lub instead of *love,*
except when she says to me
"I love you"
when love is always love.

sounds

At home, Mom and her new boyfriend, Sam, are noisy with
squeals of delight and laughter mixed with sounds of shouting,
     doors slamming, stumbles and falls
that blur pleasure and pain
until I wake to either:
          Mom and him kissing, entangled on the couch.
          Or, screaming until a fist punches a wall, or her flesh.

At Abuela's,
there is silence
except the loud thrummmmmm of the A/C
and her slight snoring on the other side of the thin wall between
     our bedrooms.

At home, in my room, I close the door, to hide under Empire
     Strikes Back sheets
from raised voices downstairs that crawl up through the air
     vents like serpents,
with the hot hot heat, filling my room
like the evil spirits that penetrate my dreams with nightmares
     of demons and kidnappers.

At Abuela's,
there is quiet
until I turn on the TV. And even then Abuela asks,
"Will you turn it down a little, por favor?"

At home, at night,
there is always noise, that keeps me awake.

At Abuela's
there is only a soft hush

until I crack the window, letting in the chirp-chirp-chirping of
    crickets
singing songs
      that I am not alone
          and that I can finally close my eyes.

wheels

In Mom's little white car. In Abuela's gray car. In Dad's blue
    truck. In Sam's littered truck. On the yellow school bus. I
    am always going somewhere . . .

. . . to Abuela's
Abilene, Texas, where we go to the library and I can eat as
    much as I want, whatever I want . . . until I have to come
    back to San Marcos and be with Mom again.

. . . to my dad's apartment
on the other side of San Marcos, which doesn't have furniture
except a mattress he found behind a dumpster and sprayed
    with Lysol so it wouldn't smell.

. . . to my mom's, which is my house, I guess,
Sam's truck smelling of stale beer from crushed cans and fresh
    smoke from Kool menthols or stinky from cigarettes he rolls
    himself from his "dime bag" that has no dimes in it.

. . . or to school
to learn big words like *vehicle* (which means cars or trucks
    or buses, or even boats and planes and trains) from Mrs.
    Hamm, who has a bag of prizes for students who behave,
    and whose husband is a magician and does magic on
    Fridays if everyone is good all week. I always try to be good,
    even when Mom or Dad or Sam say I'm bad 'cause I'm
    always in the way.

Abuela never says that.
She never says I'm in the way.
She never says that I'm bad.

But if Mom and Dad and Sam all say it,
maybe Abuela is wrong.

a see you

Abuela drives slower
and slower
and slower
until we can hear
gravel crushed and crunched, one by one, beneath her tires.

"This is where I went to college,
where I got my bachelor's in three years
my master's one year after that
while raising five children
after my husband died,
across the world,
for our country
in Vietnam.
One day, I would like you to attend here: A.C.U."

Confused, I respond
"I see you too."

"No. The school is named A.C.U. Abilene Christian
    University."
"It's for Christians?"
"Yes. It is a wonderful school with wonderful people."
"I can't go. I'm not Christian."

Abuela brakes. The car lurches to a stop,
her eyes grabbing me.
"Of course you are."

I shake my head.
"Nuh-uh. I'm not baptized.
I went to church with Robby and the preacher said you're not Christian til
    they put you under water."

"Do you want to be baptized?"

I shake my head, no.

"Mom doesn't like church. She said I'm not allowed to go with Robby anymore."

"Why not?"

"'Cause I asked if Sam moving in was living in sin, 'cause they're not married."

Abuela's lips become a thin line.

"God loves all of us. Especially children. God loves you. If you want to be a Christian, if you want to be baptized—"

"But Mom would get mad."

Abuela asks what my mom has never asked:

"What do YOU want?"

I think about it for a full minute.

"Can we have cake for dinner?"

janitor

We have walked the college campus from east to west, when
    Abuela asks,
"Do you want to see the chapel?"
I shake my head, no. *"Can we see the library instead?"*
Abuela would have preferred the chapel, but she is happy with
    my answer.
"If we hurry, they will be closing soon."

The sun sets as we walk inside.
A man looks at his watch, agitated.
When he sees my grandmother he snaps his fingers twice,
"You're late. Why aren't you in your uniform? You can't bring
    your kid here."

When I realize he is talking to Abuela, rude,
I growl, *"This's my 'Buela. She can do whatever she wants."*

The man crosses his arms, one eyebrow raised.
"Not if she wants to work here."

Abuela's confusion steps aside. She takes a breath.
"I do not work here," she explains gently. "I graduated from
    here."

"Oh," is all the man says—until another brown-skinned
    woman walks in. "There you go. You can see my error. You
    two look exactly alike."

I look at the two women.
They look nothing alike.

They wear different clothes, have different hair, even the
    browns of their skin are different.

"*They don't look alike!*" I shout,
even as Abuela steers me toward the exit.
She is quiet, even as I say again and again,
"*But you don't.*"

invisible men

In San Marcos,
Sam, Mom, and I come home
to find our apartment door wide open,
the shiny knob and lock hanging from their hole like a dead
    bird from its nest.
Muddy boot prints crisscross the carpet among overturned
    furniture
and the places where our TV and stereo sat, now dusty and
    empty.

Mom hits Sam in the chest twice,
shouting, "What'd you do? Who do you owe this time?"
Urgent, frightened, the grown man runs upstairs, looking for
    something
while Mom grabs the phone, to call the police.

Left behind, forgotten,
I stand in the doorway, confused.
It occurs to me the men who broke in must be invisible
(except for their footprints),
and turned our TV and stereo invisible too.
It's only when I walk over to the wooden shelf and reach out my
    hand that I realize
No, the TV is gone
along with Mom's pearl earrings,
Sam's cigar box of rolled up joints and dollar bills that I'm not
    supposed to know about,
and my Walkman, with my *Footloose Soundtrack* tape inside.

I think of Abuela,
who always whispers to my mom
that Sam is trouble.
I wonder to myself, if adults get spanked too,

or if that's just for kids.
I start to laugh,
until Mom grabs me and shakes me, screaming,
"This isn't funny!"

replacement

Abuela pleads with Mom for us to move to Abilene.
She says, "It is not safe for Rex there."
"It's not safe anywhere, Mother!" my mom shouts.

Abuela sends me a new Walkman. It is the same as the stolen
    one,
except it doesn't have the *Footloose* tape in it. I ask, "What will I
    dance to?"
Sam rolls his eyes. "You dance like a girl."

I smile at the compliment
                before realizing,

                it was not meant as one.

mexico (witches)

Abuela wants to see her Mamá y Papá
in Nuevo Laredo, Tamaulipas
and introduce them to her two grandsons.
So we drive to Mexico (or "Meh-hico" when Abuela says it).
We being: me, Mom, my cousin Donald, Aunt Frannie, and
    Abuela.

Eight hours
the drive is long—and hot.
The car's air-conditioning does not reach the backseat,
where sweat pours through my shirt, dripping down into my
    Spiderman Underoos.

Outside our car windows,
women on street corners sell fresh-cut papaya from small tables
men on street corners sell shaved ice with flavored syrup from
    small metal carts
children crowd street corners with extended hands,
the same brown as mine,
asking, "Uno peso uno peso por favor!"
Behind them,
pink, red, and orange adobe homes,
some with no glass in their windows, no doors in their entries
so I can peek inside and see dusty floors.
The churches stand tall,
white towers with church bells
topped by crosses,
while closer to the sidewalk
Jesus waits on his cross, watching me, his forehead bleeding
    from thorns
and his mother the Virgin Mary, painted on walls everywhere,
    hands together,
as if praying for each person that passes by.

The air shimmers with wavy lines of heat,
as if ghosts are dancing in the air
invisible to all eyes, except mine. . .

I whisper to Donald,
"Do you see the spirits?"
"No, where?"
"You can't see them. I can, 'cause I'm a witch."

Aunt Frannie says,
"You might have taken after Abuela's mother.
She was a curandero. A healer."
"She was?"
Abuela says, "She was not a bruja!"
Frannie smiles, leaning forward, one hand on her mother's
    shoulder.
"No one said she was a witch, Mom.
But she helped deliver babies, and used homemade remedies for
    healing."
"Shhh," Abuela says. "I am a Christian now."

I ask,
"Did she have powers?
Could she see things no one else could?
Could she start fires with her mind?
Did she ride a broom?
Do you think I'll have powers?!"

Abuela says, "Shush. No more nonsense.
I am driving."

mexico (heat)

It is so hot.
We are all sweating, especially Mom in her long-sleeved shirt
    and denim jeans.
I am sitting next to the right window, facing the sun as it flies
    toward the west
but still taking the time to beat down on me,
pushing through the glass, to bake me where I sit
like pan dulce in an oven.

People in the streets
their faces change, melting like candles
under a flame
my eyes growing
heavy
I ask,
"How much
longer?
I think I
need some
water."
I slump
down in my seat, unable to move,
when Frannie says,
"Rex! Rex? Give me some water, Luciana! Hurry!"
and Mom's voice is shouting,
"Rex, quit horsing around! You're not funny!"
And Abuela says, "¡Ay, Dios mío!"
pulling the car over and fanning me
saying, "He might have heatstroke!"
but everyone is far away
even Donald, who is sitting right next to me, asking,
"Is he dead?
If he is, can I use his Walkman?"

mexico (fussing)

I am overheated
but I do not have heatstroke
according to Mom
who is annoyed
Abuela is still fussing over me,
half an hour later.
"He's fine, Mother. You gave him water.
Can we start driving again? Let's just get there already.
I hate Mexico."

mexico (stores)

We walk among shops for tourists
selling brightly colored everything
painted pots and plates and piñatas hanging all over the ceiling
large guitars for adults, small guitars that a baby monkey might
    strum
maracas, which Donald and I shake as a toothless man laughs
    at us,
and mirrored crosses and burning corazones and art made of
    tin or recycled soda cans.
Sarapes and sombreros
baskets brimming with thousands of hand-woven friendship
    bracelets
(making me wish I had one thousand friends to give them to)
dresses embroidered with flowers, called huipil,
and beaded jewelry, called huichol,
hundreds of small round animals, painted as vibrant as MTV's
    logos,
dragons, dogs, snails, snakes, cats, devils, some are
    who-knows-what-kind-of-animal
with four thin legs and heads that bob, move, nod, shake, stir in
    the slightest breeze,
or when I put my lips together and blow . . .
My very favorite though are the shiny lucha libre masks
that wrestlers wear to hide their identities, like Spiderman
    hiding Peter Parker.

The same stores have bottles of fizzy flavored water
and aguas frescas with neon colors
and candy bars I have never heard of
and bags of potato chips that I have heard of, but with strange
    spicy flavors,
and grasshoppers, dried and bagged to be eaten
"For real?!"

and scorpions stuck in lollipops
"No way! Are they alive?"
and worms in bottles of tequila
"Why do adults drink that? They swallow worms?! Gross!!"
I shake at the thought of eating insects, and so
later, when we sit down at a restaurant to eat a late lunch,
I worry about what we will find
inside the enchiladas.

mexico (names)

When we meet Abuela's parents,
I do not know what to call them
so I don't call them anything
as I duck behind Abuela and hide.
With tender care, Abuela urges me forward to introduce
   myself.
My great-grandmother says,
"Me llamo Ignacia."
My great-grandfather says,
"Me nombre es Andres."
They admire me
without touching (at first)
like I am a doll made of glass or gold
or porcelain, easy to break, fragile.
But their eyes smile with pride, as though they had a hand in
   making me.
More people come: Consuela, José, Miguel, Isabella, Esteban,
   Francesca, Pilar, Ángel, Carmen.
There are too many to remember, so I stay close to those I
   know speak English,
even as Frannie waves for me to meet new tías and tíos and
   primos and other relatives.
Abuela's baby sister, Panny, stays at Abuela's side,
hugging her again and again and again, saying, "I miss you,
   Catalina."
I say, *"She can't move here, she has to stay living near me."*
Everyone laughs, though I don't see what's funny,
so I get mad, crossing my arms in defiance,
like my mom, who sits in the corner, talking to no one.
I listen to these strangers who share my blood,
wondering at the familiarity when they say Catalina
with the same familiarity that I say Abuela
and my mom calls her Mom.

Meaning that this woman has three names
while I only have one.

This is the first time I meet her family.

And the last time.

mexico (español)

There are many members of our extended family at the
     reunion
but I cannot understand them
because all of them speak Spanish
and I do not.
I ask Mom,
"Why don't we speak Spanish?"
"We don't need to. Everyone speaks English in the United
     States."
"What if I want to know Spanish?"
Mom rolls her eyes. "Then talk to your grandmother. She'd
     love that."

mexico (food)

There is so much food and so much music, and so many hugs.
We sleep in the living room,
with no air-conditioning
and two fans
oscillating back and forth
to blow away the hot hot heat
that returns when the fans turn their heads away.

In the morning,
Ignacia makes breakfast tacos of
huevos y papas y tocino y queso.
The juicy bits run down my chin, my neck, inside my too-big
    shirt, tickling me into laughter.
When I am done, I ask for seconds.
Abuela kisses the back of each of my hands, saying,
"There isn't any. But we will get you more food soon."

Panny hugs Abuela and they whisper
like Frannie and Mom whisper
'cause I guess sisters whisper
making me wish for a sister to whisper with.

Abuela would like to stay another night.
Donald and I clap and say yes! Frannie says yes too.
But my mom says, "No. You said two days. It's been three.
    We're leaving."
She hasn't smiled since we arrived.

I don't know why
Mom is mad all the time
but I suspect it has to do with the bruises
colored like plum and yellow squash and bright red
    poppies

that hide beneath her long-sleeved shirts and denim jeans,
gifts from Sam
so she does not forget him.

tennessee

I am going to visit my grandparents, to my dad's parents,
to their home in the Smoky Mountains,
for the whole summer.
At the airport, Abuela hugs me, whispering, "I wish you could
    stay with me,
but it is not far enough away from Sam."
She kisses my ear so hard, it pops.
She wipes away her tears, forcing a smile that I know isn't true.
"Go. Be happy. Te amo siempre."

I don't want to go. But it might be good
for Mom, who says my laugh hurts her ears.
Sam hurts her enough. I don't want to hurt her too.

I don't want to go so far away though.
Mom needs me. Her eyes say it.
Even if she refuses to hug me before I get on the plane.

In the sky, aboard a plane full of people, I fly alone,
trying not to cry.
The stewardess brings me ginger ale, pretzels, and a flight pin
shaped like a tiny airplane.

In Tennessee,
I see my younger cousin, Dani, pretty in her pink dress.
My aunt Kelly, who makes us pray before every meal.
Her husband, who rides a motorcycle.
My grandmother June, who always asks me to sit in her lap,
and loves me through and through, the way Abuela loves me.
And my grandfather, who looks at me like a stranger in his
    house and says,
again and again,
"I don't care much for your mother."

third

My grandfather's name is also Rex,
like my dad,
like me.

Here, in Sevierville,
everyone calls my grandfather Rex,
because he is the first Rex.
They call my dad Buster,
even though he is the second Rex.
And they call me, the third Rex,
Bubba.

The first week, I try to correct everyone.
"My name is Rex."
Until my grandfather stares down at me, his eyes cold as ice,
"Defiant. Just like your mother. Are you going to scream like
    her too?
Pitch a tantrum? Make a scene?"

I whisper, *"No."*
For the rest of the summer,
I whisper.
Because I don't want anyone to think
that I am anything like my mom.

june

Instead of "Bubba,"
the neighbor kids call me "Rice and Beans"
until I run home.

Grandma June finds me hiding under the back porch,
wiping the tears from my brown cheeks.
"Ignore them," she says. "There is nothing wrong with being
    different."

She pats her lap. I crawl into it. She hugs me hard, sniffing me,
    saying,
"I've always loved the way you smell. Ever since you were a
    baby."
From a leather case, she pulls a cigarette, puts it between her
    lips, and lights it.

She smokes one after another, as she rocks me, telling me I was
    her first grandchild,
that I have a special place in her heart, which is why she was
    glad when Abuela called,
and asked if I could come visit.
"You spoke with Abuela?"
June nods. "She's the one who paid for your plane ticket here."

That night, in the cold Tennessee basement where I sleep,
I am warm, thinking of Abuela,
whose love I can feel,
all the way from Texas.

gone

When I go back to Abilene,
the first time since Tennessee,
Mom doesn't go inside.

As soon as I step out of the car, she drives away.
I walk the last steps up to 1214 South Jackson Drive, alone, and
    ring the doorbell.

"Where is your mom?" Abuela asks.
"She left."
"And your clothes?"
"She drove off."
"Did she even say good-bye?"
I shake my head, no.

Abuela closes her eyes, takes a long breath, then hugs me.
"It is better this way."
She doesn't let go for a long time.

gum

Wrigley's Doublemint gum,
flat sticks, dusted in powder, wrapped in paper (foil on the
    outside, white paper on the in),
Abuela always has it
in her purse
in her car
on her desk
in her kitchen
so that she can always offer me one.

She unwraps it, like corn on the cob, fresh from the farm,
shucking the gum at the top,
peeling paper back and down (like a superhero's cape),
then holding it out, for me to bite away
no dirty fingers to sully the prize.

I chew and chew and chew
the peppermint
cooling my tongue
sweetening my breath
trying to blow bubbles
before the gum hardens in my mouth from too much chewing
which is when Abuela
(somehow she always knows)
holds out her hand.

Into her palm I spit
the now-flavorless wad of corn syrup
as she digs into her purse to find its original wrapper
and return the gum from where it came,
wrapping it in the foil paper, a round ball, and squeezing it flat,
then dropping it into her purse
like a valued coin
to spend later.

the mall

When I visit Abilene,
Abuela takes me to Dyess Air Force Base (no tax!)
where I pick out one LEGO set,
and to the Abilene Mall,
to my favorite place in the world to eat:
Chick-fil-A.

Back home, Mom always says,
"It's too expensive!
Just eat the free samples!"
And I do,
devouring the single salty chicken nugget at the end of a
    toothpick,
before asking the woman politely,
"Can I have one more?"

But in Abilene,
with Abuela,
we wait in line, my shoes slipping and sliding on the greasy
    tiled floor,
as Abuela whispers, "You can get whatever you want."

I know I will get waffle fries and a Coke.
But the struggle for me, each and every time
(since I come here so seldom):
Do I get the chicken sandwich
with its fried breast on sweet buttered bread buns with two,
    maybe three, pickle slices?
Or do I get the chicken nuggets
fried so perfectly, golden brown, full of mouth-watering juicy
    flavor
and sometimes a few little crunchy bits at the bottom?

The nuggets win out once again.
When I take the red tray and sit at the table,
I cannot wait to open the small white box with red letters,
    which to me is a treasure chest,
full of joy, born from an empty stomach.

latchkey kid

Abuela sends my mom a monthly check for day care.
Mom deposits the check and tells me,
"You're old enough to come home straight after school. To take
    care of yourself."
I agree. I am eight and a half.
Practically an adult.

Each day, after school, I ride the bus to the stop off the
    highway,
where I get off with the other kids.
Tammy and Chris and Mike wave and leave me at the trailer
    park.
I walk the rest of the way to my apartment complex alone.
I take the key from my necklace, and open the door.

I am free. No Mom. No Sam.

They won't be home until late,
which means hours of cartoons, MTV, and homework
before I make my own dinner.

I need to stand on a chair, but making food is fun.
I can make hot dogs.
Scrambled eggs.
Grilled cheese.
SpaghettiOs.
I can even do Kraft mac and cheese, though I always make a
    mess with the orange powder, which makes Mom angry, if I
    don't clean it all up.

I like being a latchkey kid.
Only one rule, Mom says.
"Don't tell Abuela."

rounder

Mom's belly grows rounder
and rounder, pushing out,
like a balloon under her shirt.

I think Mom is getting fat,
until she and Sam,
filled to brimming with excitement,
tell me,
"You're going to be a big brother!"

Their joy waits for mine, but nothing comes.
I think, *I like being the only child.*
Mom grows angry, waiting for my joy.
She shakes me, shouting,
"Aren't you excited?!"

I shrug.
I won't know til they're here.

brother

I sit on the sidewalk in San Marcos, Texas,
and wait,
chin in palms, elbows on knees, bare feet
on the apartment parking lot asphalt.

When Abuela arrives, I run to her car door
to get the first hug.
"I love you I love you I love you
Let's go somewhere else!"
Abuela smiles.
"May I meet your brother first?"
"No. He's loud. He cries all the time.
And he poops himself.
Mom made me change his diaper and the poop smelled.
And he peed on me."

Abuela smiles tenderly, giggles with care.
"Your caca smelled too.
And you peed on me once. A few times actually."
"No I didn't!"
"You did. But I still love you. Te amo siempre."
"Promise?"
"I promise. May I meet Ford now?"
"I guess.
His name is stupid.
Sam named him after a car."

I watch Abuela holding my brother.
She rocks him, cradles him,
and I wish I were little again,
so she would rock and cradle me.

So I get mad,
and leave.

When Abuela finally finds me
sitting under a tree, on the other side of the apartment complex,
gently pulling caterpillars from bark so they'll inch and twist up
   my arm,
she says, "Hola, mijo."
I say nothing, staring at the ground.
"You will like your brother one day."
"No I won't."
"You will."
"How do you know?"
"Because I had six brothers. And six sisters."
"You did?!"
She shakes her head. "One was adopted,
Javier, who my mom adopted after his mother died giving birth."
"That's . . . (hold on, I'm counting . . .) thirteen kids in one house?!"
"Yes. My twin is my closest brother."
"You're a twin?!"
My brain wiggles and twists, like the caterpillar on my arm,
from this new story about Abuela, who I thought I knew so well
because she belongs to me.
She also belongs (I suppose) to her own five children
and two grandsons—
three grandsons now.
"I didn't know you had so many brothers and sisters."
Abuela nods, saying,
"And now you have one.
Sometimes you will like your brother. Sometimes you will not.
But you will love him. And he will love you.
You are hermanos.
Take care of each other."
"Okay . . ." I finally say,
" . . . *but only if I stay your favorite."*
She smirks, then winks.
"Por supuesto."

bad friends

I am in the parking lot with Mike and Chris
Playing G.I. Joe's with our little toy men with rifles and knives,
when Abuela comes out to see me.
She kisses my ears *POP*! *POP*!
and I take her hand and pull her to meet my friends
from the trailer park next door.
I say with pride, *"This is my Abuela."*
Mike snorts. Chris laughs. "Ebola?"
"Abuela. It's Spanish for Grandma."
"So just call her Grandma," Mike says.
"Hello, young men," Abuela says, her *y* like a *j*.
"Did you say *jung?*" Mike asks.
Chris says, slowly and loudly, "HO-LA, OLD LADY."
Mike and Chris both crack up.
My whole body heats until I growl, *"Shut up."*

Chris gives me his middle finger,
then pushes Mike away from me and Abuela.
"Let's get outta here."
"Yeah, let's leave Rex alone with his *ebola*."
"It's Abuela!" I shout.
After they pocket their action figures,
they hop on their bikes and pedal away.

Abuela says, "Your friends are very rude."
"You're rude," I snap, yanking my hand from hers.
I blame her, though I don't know why.

The rest of her visit, I stay mad.
I call her Grandma instead of Abuela because
all I can hear is the way she says *jes* instead of *yes*,
as if reminding me, being different is wrong.

jokes

The next time I see Mike and Chris,
we are on the school bus
I go to sit with them. They say,
"Uh-uh."
"No way."
"Why not?"
"We don't sit with beaners."
"Or spics."
"What's that?"
"That's you, you and your *ebola*."
Others around us laugh.
My body grows hot . . .

Even though I sit two rows away, I can still hear them the
    whole ride to school,
"*J*es, Rex is a *j*ung man. One day, he will work a *y*ob as a
    dishwasher."
"Or sell flowers on the side of the road."
       . . . and hotter . . .

"Knock knock."
"Who's there?"
"Orange."
"Orange who?"
"Orange you glad you're not a wetback, like Rex?"
       . . . and hotter . . .

"How many people in Rex's family does it take to put in a light
    bulb?"
"Doesn't matter. They're too short."
         . . . and hotter . . .

"Why does Rex's ebola refry her beans?"

"Ever heard of Mexicans doing things right the first time?"
                    . . . and hotter . . .

"What's Rex's favorite sport?"
"What?"
"Cross country. 'Cause border crossing isn't a sport."
                              . . . and hotter . . .

                    . . . til the whole world turns red.
I stand
walking back to Mike and Chris, even as the bus driver yells,
    "Sit down!"
and since Chris is sitting closest to the aisle,

              I punch him as hard as I can in his face.

It is not the first time
I have been in the principal's office
                    for fighting

                    and it will not be the last.

tortillas

The Garcias are our neighbors.
They live in the same complex
in an apartment just like ours
except backward—like a mirror reflection.
The two bedrooms and one bathroom and the kitchen are all
    the exact same—
except facing the opposite direction.
Plus, they have seven people living there—the four kids, Mamá
    y Papá, and their abuela.
They have a small Mexican restaurant in a strip mall,
where Mom takes me on Sundays.
She and Mrs. Garcia go next door to get their nails done.
I stay with Alejandra, Juan, Carlos, and Isabella.
We do our homework, or color in coloring books,
or play Monopoly (though some of the pieces are missing),
and watch their own abuela in the kitchen, rolling small dough
    balls,
then smashing them down into round disk after round disk
    after round disk,
before placing them on a pan over a flame,
so that they rise with brown crisp bubbles—white with brown
    flecks—thinner than paper,
until one of us kids
steals one of the disks
(tossing it from one hand to the other, *hot hot hot!* dusting our
    fingers in powder)
and runs back to the table
where we slather it with butter
or honey
and cinnamon
and devour it
like wolves.

tex-mex

"Abuela, why do you never make me fresh tortillas?"
"It is hard work."
"Why do you not make enchiladas at home?
Or flautas?
Or sopapillas?
Like Abuela Tejerrina?"
"It is too much work for one person. I live alone. I prefer TV
    dinners."
"Didn't you grow up eating Tex-Mex?"
Abuela shakes her head. "No. Tex-Mex only exists in the
    United States.
In Mexico, it is just called food. Comida."
"Did your mom not teach you to make comida?"
"She did. But only arroz y frijoles
and sometimes tortillas,
but only on special occasions when we had enough flour for
    dough.
Usually we did not. We never had big meals. There were no
    feasts.
We were too poor."

interruption

My fourth-grade teacher is teaching science
by pouring vinegar into a volcano
making red lava bubbles bubble out
when an aide knocks and interrupts the class.
"Rex Ogle? You need to go to the principal's office."
The students go, "Ooooooooooooh! You're in trouble."

Outside the office, my mom waits
sitting on a red student chair, too small for her adult body.
She takes my hand and says, "Let's go."
"Where are we going?"
"Colorado."
"To visit?"
"To live."

Outside the school, our truck waits,
Sam in the driver's seat, Ford in his baby seat, the last seat
    waiting for Mom.
I have to crawl into a small space in the back of the camper
    shell,
between the boxes of our belongings.
"Wait. Are we going home first?"
"No. We have everything we need."
"But what about all my stuff? My books? My toys?"
"You'll get new stuff."

"Can't I say good-bye to my friends?"
"You can call them when we get there."
"Wait. How far is Colorado from Abuela?"
My mom rolls her eyes.
"Who cares?"

I do.

collect call

I dial 0.

The operator says, "How may I direct your call?"

"I need to place a collect call."

Abuela accepts the charges.

"Are you okay? I have been calling but your phone is
disconnected."

"We're not home anymore. In Texas I mean."

"Where are you?"

"Boulder, Colorado."

"¿Qué? Why are you there?"

*"Mom moved us. I didn't know. One day she just showed up at school.
She left almost all my toys behind. All I have left is the Millennium
Falcon."*

"Where are you now?"

"At a pay phone. Outside my new school."

Abuela whispers on the other end. I am not sure if they are
prayers or curses.

"Did your mom say why she left?"

*"She said there were no jobs in San Marcos.
That her and Sam would get jobs here.
But they haven't. They're really mad."*

"Where are you living?"

*"With the Garcias. They moved here last month. But the trailer is too
small for eleven of us.
I want to come back. Can I come live with you?"*

"If your mom will let you," Abuela says,
"but she won't."

I hear her crying on the other end of the phone line.

interruption #2

My new fourth-grade teacher is teaching music
by letting us watch people singing in
The Sound of Music
when an aide knocks and interrupts the class.
"Rex Ogle? You need to go to the principal's office."
The students go, "Ooooooooooooh! You're in trouble."

Outside the office, my mom waits
standing in a pair of baggy sweats, too big for her body.
She takes my hand and says, "Let's go."
"Where are we going?"
"Back to Texas."
"To visit?"
"To live."

Outside the school, our truck waits,
Sam in the driver's seat, Ford in his baby seat, the last seat
    waiting for Mom.
I have to crawl into a medium space in the back of the camper
    shell,
where there are fewer things than last time.
"Wait. Are we going home to San Marcos?"
"No. We're going to Paris, to live with Sam's brother."
"Paris, France?!"
"No, dummy. Paris, Texas."

"Are we saying bye to the Garcias?"
"No. They're liars and thieves."
"Wait. How far is Paris from Abuela?"
My mom rolls her eyes.
"Who cares?"

I do.

collect call #2

I dial 0.

The operator says, "How may I direct your call?"

"I need to place a collect call."

Abuela accepts the charges.

"Are you okay?"

"I'm fine."

"Thank God. Thank goodness you are alright. Where are you now?"

"Paris."

"Paris, France?"

"No, dummy. Paris, Texas."

"Rex. Do not call me a dummy. It is disrespectful."

"Sorry."

"Where are you now?"

"At a pay phone. Outside my new school."

"Where are you living?"

"With Sam's brother, his wife, their kids, and Ford's grandpa Luther.

He's always drunk though.

Last night he peed the couch while he was sleeping."

Abuela whispers on the other end. I am not sure if they are prayers or curses.

"At least you are back in Texas."

"Sam's family is annoying. Their apartment is too small for nine of us.

I have to sleep on the floor by the door. It's cold.

Can I come live with you?"

"If your mom will let you," Abuela says,

"but she won't."

I hear her sniffling on the other end of the phone line.

interruption #3

My new fourth-grade teacher is teaching slow dancing
by making boys partner with girls
and dance slowly in a circle, hips an arm's length apart,
when an aide knocks and interrupts the class.
"Rex Ogle? You need to go to the principal's office."
The students go, "Ooooooooooh! You're in trouble."

I wave, saying, *"Good-bye. I'll never see y'all again!"*
I kiss Shanna, my dance partner, a peck on the cheek, and run out.

Outside the office, my mom waits
tapping her shoe against the linoleum floor, annoyed.
I walk past her and ask,
"Where are we going this time?"
"How did you know we're leaving?"
"I'm no dummy."

Outside the school, our truck waits,
Sam in the driver's seat, Ford in his baby seat, the last seat waiting
    for Mom.
I have to crawl into a large space in the back of the camper shell,
where there is almost nothing.
"So, where's the next stop?"
"Grapevine. And don't be a smart-ass."
"But I am smart, and I have an ass."
My mom reaches back, swatting at me. She can't reach me. I laugh
    at her.

"How far is Grapevine from Abuela?"
My mom takes a deep breath.
"Three hours."

I'm excited to see Abuela again.

collect call #3

I dial 0.

The operator says, "How may I direct your call?"

"I need to place a collect call."

Abuela accepts the charges.

"Are you okay?"

"Better than okay! We're in Grapevine!"

"You are so close now!"

"Will you come visit?"

"If your mom lets me."

"She will. She needs to borrow money."

vista nueva

Outside, our new apartment
is painted a faded turquoise and dark maroon,
like a sad Christmas.
Inside is painted dim white with beige carpet
stained and pocked with burns.

This is a two-bedroom, one-bath, under four hundred square
     feet,
which seems like a lot
since there's only four of us now
(along with the cockroaches
but they only come out at night).

Ford sleeps with Mom and Sam,
and I get my own room.
I don't have any furniture, or belongings
except a sleeping bag, my Millennium Falcon, and *Alice in
     Wonderland*,
so my room feels huge.

3
GIFTS AND FISTS

trunk

When Abuela comes to visit,
Ford and I run to the parking lot to greet her
with smiles and hugs
begging for her keys
so we can open the back of her car.

Like Santa, she comes bearing gifts,
her trunk full to the brim
with new shoes, new clothes, shampoo and soap,
Pringles and Pop-Tarts and Cheetos and Cheerios and variety
    packs of sugar cereal,
loaves of bread, peanut-butter and jelly (grape and strawberry),
Hamburger Helper, cartons of Kraft macaroni and cheese,
    packets of Rice-A-Roni,
and microwave popcorn,
bags of pretzels and chips, both potato and corn,
jars of salty nuts,
labeled with a gentleman peanut wearing a top hat, a monocle,
    and fancy shoes . . .
all of this in gray plastic bags labeled "Dyess Air Force Base,"
the place where I was born.

My mom stands in the apartment, arms crossed, angry,
saying, "I don't need you to buy us groceries, Mother,"
while Ford and I cart in bag after bag after bag,
with me saying, "Yes, you do.
Now say gracias."

Mom says nothing.

moved

The next time Abuela is allowed to visit,
we have moved again.
From the nice side of Grapevine, to the other.
Government-subsidized housing next to train tracks.
Four times a day, loud horns bellow,
our windows vibrating in sync with giant cars dragged by a
    metal engine.

"It's very nice," Abuela says again and again
even though it's not.
We have traded
a second-story home with a balcony for a second-story home
    with no balcony,
stained beige carpet for stained gray carpet with a strange
    smell,
a swimming pool for a playground made of painted tractor
    tires,
and cockroaches for ants and wasps and hornets, quick to sting.

Still, Abuela offers only compliments:
"Rex is now walking distance from middle school."
"You have windows on two sides, which means a nice breeze."
"This kitchen is much nicer than the last one."
"The rent is a good price."

Later, when we are alone, I ask,
"Why do you do that? Say only nice things? This place is a dump.
We had to move here 'cause Mom and Sam are both unemployed."
"I am positive because it does not help to be negative.
Sometimes you must focus on the good things.
Focus on what you have,
not on what you don't.""

But no matter how hard I try,
all I can focus on is
all the things
we do not have.

hunger pains

When Abuela's food runs out,
when our pantry shelves are empty,
between WIC coupons and food stamps,
my stomach sings a low song of
rumbles and grumbles
a kind of tune
that lasts all day,
and through the night,
like a jazz melody
with no rhythm.

package

In the mailbox,
a brown box arrives with my name on it
labeled in Abuela's pleasant stick-figure handwriting.
I open it in the breezeway,
suspecting but not knowing yet,
that it is exactly what I had hoped for . . .

Pecans from her trees,
plucked with love,
and sent to me
to feed
both my stomach
                    and my heart.

catalog

Today when I check the mail
I find another package from Abuela.
A catalog
from Dyess Air Force Base
filled with furniture.
Her note says,
"Let me buy some furniture for your home."

In my room, I spend hours
thumbing through each and every page,
drawing circles with my pen,
bending page corners down to remember:
mattresses,
bed frames,
bookshelves,
and desks.

Mom comes home to find me,
overjoyed and hopeful, looking forward to an apartment with
    furniture
not found behind a dumpster or purchased second-hand from
    yard sales or pawn shops.
My excitement grates her,
until she is shrieking, "Who does she think she is?!"
"Abuela just wants to help us."
"No, she's deceitful and manipulative!"
"How is she trying to deceive us? Manipulate us into what?"
"You think she's such an angel. She's not!"
"She is! You're just jealous."

When Mom tries to wrestle the catalog from my hands,
I hold tight, wrapping myself around it
protecting my dreams with my body

while Ford cries somewhere behind us
as Mom grabs me by the hair
lets her fist fly, coming down again and again
earning me the trophy
of a black eye
that will debut tomorrow
when I wake
before school.

After the scuffle, Mom takes the book of images,
ripping out page after page
tossing them into the air
making it snow
with my silly ideas
of being like my friends
with homes that look like pictures in a catalog.

furniture

When the delivery men arrive at our front door,
Mom signs on the dotted line.
In comes:
a wooden dining room table
and matching wooden chairs,
a blue sofa wrapped in plastic,
a pink chair soft like velvet,
a double mattress for Mom and Sam
and a single mattress
just for me.

After the plastic is removed,
everything placed where it will go,
Mom asks me, "It's nice, isn't it?"
But my arms are crossed,
and I refuse to smile.
"What is wrong with you? Why are you pouting?! I thought
    you wanted all this?"
"You beat me when I showed you the furniture."
"I changed my mind!!" she screams.
Then takes a deep breath. Calms
and sits on the couch that Abuela bought.

Mom rolls her eyes.
"And I barely hit you. Stop being so dramatic."

jobs

Mom has me call Abuela to thank her for the furniture.
She does not answer when I call collect.
Two days later, when I call again, I ask,
"I've called a bunch of times. Where were you?"
"At work," she says, "at one of my jobs."
"How many jobs do you have?"
"During the weekdays, I am a diagnostician for Abilene I.S.D.
Weekday evenings, I do translations for the court system,
for prisoners who cannot speak English.
After that, I teach reading and writing at the local prison.
Some nights I volunteer at the YWCA.
On the weekends I volunteer at the Senior Center, the soup kitchen,
   or church.
Or make extra money mending."
"Mending?"
"Sewing buttons or patching holes on clothes."
"You have . . ." I count, *"eight jobs?!"*
"I work because I can. I use the extra money to buy my children and
   grandchildren
whatever they need, like furniture,
then send the rest to my family in Mexico.
When I first married, I worked every day, doing anything I could—
   mending, laundry, cleaning houses, scrubbing toilets—to make a
   little extra, to send home, to help my parents,
to help put my twin brother through medical school.
Now he is a doctor."
I ask again, *"You have eight jobs?!"*

I wonder:
How does an old woman have eight jobs,
while my mom, a young woman,
and my stepdad, a young man,
have zero jobs
between the two of them?

bars

The next time we visit
1214 South Jackson Drive,
it is the same:
red bricks
with white trim
white wood beams
a white tin roof,
but now
with white bars over the windows.

"Abuela! It's like being in jail," I say. *"Why did you get bars on your*
windows?"
"My neighborhood is not as safe as it used to be."
"Can't you just move somewhere safer?"
"I could, but I won't,"
Abuela says,
"Because I am saving money for you to go to college."

grades

When I see Abuela,
I show her my report card
to show that I am trying hard to earn
my five A's, my two B's, and my high C in English,
which is only a C because the teacher does not like me.

"Those are wonderful grades," Abuela says.
"No, they're not," my mom says, "they're average."
Abuela asks me, "Did you do your best?"
I nod, yes.
"Yeah, right," Mom says.
"Luciana," Abuela addresses her daughter, "he did his best."
Mom sneers. "What that report card doesn't say is he got
    caught fighting. Again!
He's been suspended. Twice!"

I do not want Abuela to know the bad things about me.
I yell at my mom, "*Shut up!*"

Like a lioness, Mom leaps on top of me.
Like an eagle, she grabs a chunk of my arm,
twists it in her talons until I wince in agony.
Like a gorilla, she rises up, sneering, "Don't take that tone with me!"
I shout back, unafraid, "*This is the tone you talk to me with all the time!*"
Mom slaps me, once, hard, across the face.
"You little brat!"
I scream back, "*I hate you!*"

Abuela sits very still, shaking,
until she raises her voice, "Stop it! Both of you!"

Then she goes to her room
and cries.

books on tape (again)

When Ford and I come to visit,
there is a cassette player in my room
with a shiny gold sticker: Property of Abilene Public Library.
Ford asks, "For music?"
"No. Abuela borrowed it from the library.
So you can listen to books on tape."
"Books on tape?"
In his eyes, I can see
him trying to imagine pictures made of sound,
like I once did,
which does not work.
I take his hand, and say,
"Let's go to the library.
I'll show you."

boo! (again)

I slide the tape into the cassette player
and press PLAY.
Ford crawls into my lap
as the book in my hands comes to life,
haunting music in the air,
and the ghost saying, "oooooooooooooh . . ."

A shiver runs through me,
recalling how this book made me feel
when I was young.
I grin for those days
(when crayons made me happy)
that seem so far away, so long ago,
yet so close.

My brother buries his head
in my chest,
his smothered voice crying,
"Turn it off! Turn it off!
It's scary!"

Remembering,
I carry the book
and the tape
and put them both in the freezer.

backyard (#2)

Jason's house is across South Jackson Drive from Abuela's.
It is one story,
painted yellow, though the paint is peeling,
flaking into the yellow grass
with a wheel-less truck parked in the front yard
on cinder blocks.

I ring the doorbell.
Jason's mom answers the door, a cigarette between her fingers.
I ask,
"Is Jason here?"
Jason appears behind his mother,
taller now, still with sandy hair and green eyes, a smile
with crooked teeth like mine.
He waves me inside
his home darker and dirtier than I remember.
But we do not stay inside,
in the air-conditioning.
Jason slides open the glass door
then the screen door
and reveals his backyard
under the bright sun.

Rusted chains on swings, faded color of a slide baked under the
     sun,
cat feces half-buried in the sandbox along with old beer bottles
     and cigarettes butts,
a nest of brown recluse spiders playing along the dirt floor of an
     ignored treehouse,
water-wilted pornographic magazines of naked women
stored on the top shelf of the cabinet
full of dirty and broken toys
forgotten by both
time and Jason.

We aren't children anymore
the backyard wonderland has lost its shine and luster
as we sit in plastic chairs, talking awkwardly, with long pauses,
trying to recall
why we were friends.

at church (again)

At church,
for some reason,
Ford and I always giggle and laugh,
when everyone bows their heads in prayer,
as if we cannot control ourselves, when everyone is quiet.

Abuela hushes us,
"Be respectful,"
and pinches (not too hard)
where my butt cheek meets my thigh
which only makes me
laugh
harder.

clothes

The clothes at Dyess Air Force Base don't have any brands that
    I know.
I say, *"I don't like these."*
"They are made in the U.S.A.," Abuela says, "They are top
    quality."
She holds up a shirt. "How about this one?"
Wearing this, I will be mocked at school,
and I want so desperately to look like my tormentors.
"Ew. Gross. Can we go to the mall?"
Mom says, "You're so spoiled."
I mumble, *"Yeah, right."*
Mom snaps, "What was that?"
Abuela says, "Let's go to the mall."

At the Abilene mall,
they have the stores where my peers shop in Dallas—
Ocean Pacific, The Gap, Lucky Brand, Doc Martens,
    Gadzooks, Hot Topic, JCPenny.
I believe if Abuela buys me the right clothes that I might be
    popular and cool
that I will no longer wear a target on my back.
When Abuela sees the price tag, she whispers,
"You can get more clothes for less money at the Air Force
    Base."
I whisper, *"But I want these. Por favor, Abuela. Por favor."*
But when Abuela goes to the cash register,
Mom sees the total and shouts,
"Uh-uh!" and, "No way!"
She starts shouting at me, and I start shouting back
until Abuela's face turns red and she walks out of the store
out of the mall
and goes to wait for us
in her car
under the hot Texas sun.

comics

"Does Abilene have a comic book store?"
Abuela says, "If there is, I will take you."

In the phone book's yellow pages, I find the address,
writing the numbers and street down on the back of an
    envelope
and present it to Abuela.
She nods.

We return,
Abuela with her black leather purse, eighteen dollars lighter,
and me with a brown paper bag held in my arms like a dear
    child,
with stories to help me escape my reality.

When Mom returns from Aunt Frannie's to pick me up,
she finds me nestled in bed, carefully
turning page after page,
soaking up bright colors and action and words
like a sponge that has found its way back to the sea
after a long time in the desert.

Mom's voice, shrill, to Abuela, "Did you buy those for him?!"
"He likes to read."
"Those aren't books!! He can't learn anything from those!!"
"He enjoys them. Let him read."
"They're trash!!"
"But he is reading,"
Abuela says, her voice lowering with each response.

She bows her head,
as if this will appease my mom.

But nothing will.

sneaky

When we are leaving,
Mom does not hug Abuela
or thank her for the bounty we've received.
Instead, she goes and sits in the car, and turns on the engine.

Abuela hugs Ford,
who runs after Mom,
like a baby, because he's still only four, and
Sam and Mom never hit him. He's too precious, I guess.

Abuela hugs me,
pulling me in close, her lips at my ear,
whispering, "For every A you make in school, I will give you
    five dollars.
For every A+, I will give you ten."

"Abuela, you don't have to—"
"Shhh. Good grades are important.
Very important for your future. And you are smart,
no matter what your mom says."

"No, I'm not. I'm not smart.
Not like the other kids at my school."
"If you are not smarter," Abuela says, "then work harder.
Your future is what you make it."

HONK!!
Mom lays on her horn, shouting out the window, "Come on
    already!"

Abuela slips a crumpled twenty-dollar bill into my palm with a
    sly smirk,
closing my hand shut, her hand over my mine, squeezing.

"Abuela, you don't—"
"I want to," she whispers, "you are worth investing in. You are
    special.
One day, you will do great things.
If you work hard."

HONK!! HONK!!!!
Mom slaps her horn again and again, shouting out the window,
   "I'm going to leave you!"

"Go," Abuela says. "Te amo siempre."

In the car, I hold the twenty-dollar bill in my hand,
hiding it from my mother, who yells about traffic.
The cash damp from Abuela's sweat,
letting me know that she worked hard for it

                            and I should too.

christmas dinner

This holiday,
Abuela comes to visit us.
I insist she sleep in my bed,
since she paid for it.
The next day, we have the conversation we have every year.
"I'm not cooking!" Mom snaps.
"*I'll cook*," I say.
"No one's cooking. It's expensive."
"I'll pay for the groceries," Abuela says.
"No! I don't want a mess in my kitchen. We'll go out to eat!"

We go to Luby's,
a cafeteria for old people,
which has better food than the cafeteria at my school
because they have everything, and you can choose,
chicken parmesan or Salisbury steak
mashed potatoes or French fries
creamed corn or creamed spinach
cornbread or dinner rolls
Jell-O or cheesecake
or ice cream
or one of everything

because Abuela is paying.

electric toothbrush

When I open the lush wrapping,
my joy melts into confusion.
"An electric toothbrush?"
Abuela smiles, "It is what dentists recommend."
This is the first gift she has ever given me that I want to return.

"Promise me you will use it."
"Maybe."
She opens her mouth, pointing, almost counting each white
    tooth to me.
"I have all my teeth. If you use that toothbrush,
when you are my age, you will have all your teeth too.
You will thank me."
I think the gift is stupid.

But I use it,
just in case.

journal

In the bookstore,
I hold it, turning it over and over
examining the gold edges of each page,
the strings and glue binding them together
the straight lines on the paper,
though barely visible,
on which I imagine my block handwriting
creating ideas on paper,
like Shakespeare, Dickens, Stoker, or the woman who wrote
    Frankenstein,
Mary Shelley, only eighteen, a genius.
If I write in a journal, my ideas might bloom
like a garden of stories,
to make my life worth something,

To matter,
to be someone
more than my mother's son,
or my father's forgotten child,
more than a punching bag of bruises,
more than the butt of jokes at school where my lunch is free.

I want my words, my life, to mean something . . .

Abuela watches me with the book, and walks over,
"Do you want this?"
I return it to the shelf. The brown leather binding. The hard
    cover. The gold trim.
It is not worth a fight with Mom.
"It's too expensive."
She shakes her head. "A book is priceless."
My heart races as she takes it to the counter,

scanning the aisles for my mother, a ballistic missile that seeks
    to destroy.
Abuela offers money to the cashier,
and I feel sick to my stomach, ready to retch,
worried this will cause a fight—
my desire to matter.

The journal sneaks into Abuela's purse,
a secret between her keys and the foil-paper gum wrappers
crinkled around gum chewed in my mouth.

Later, Mom will discover it,
this secret, between *her* mother and *her* son
(because we belong to *her*)
and she will riot
and shout, throwing the book at me,
screaming,
"Why would you spend twenty dollars on a book with no words
    in it?!"

When I scream back,
"*'Cause I want to put MY words in it,*"
her fist will meet my jaw,
in front of Abuela who will clutch her own face,
as though she were struck.

While Abuela cries quietly, begging my mom not to hit me
    again,
I will shout,
"*These are my words! They matter! Hit me all you want! I will write!*"

These are my words.
They do matter.
And she did hit me, all she wanted.
But I wrote.

And I still write.
      I will always write.
            No one can stop me from writing.

My words are mine,
with a voice given to me
by my abuela.

4

AN EDUCATION

español

In high school,
students may choose three electives each semester,
one must be a foreign language.

On the couch, Mom flips through magazines
saying, "Take Latin. It's the basis for all languages.
Or French. Girls love romantic languages."
My head shakes right to left to right.
"No. I want to take Spanish,
so I can speak with Abuela in her first language."
Mom's spine goes erect, snapping to attention
like a scorpion's tale . . .
"No. I forbid it."

So dramatic, the word "forbid," I think of cartoons and
a chuckle escapes my throat.
Mom leaps across the room
an olive-skinned jaguar
snatching my arm and squeezing,
"I said, NO!"

Later,
before I lick the envelope closed,
before I place an American bald eagle stamp to fly my letter to
    its destination,
I take the class selection form
scribbling black ink over the word "Latin"
in Mom's tall loops of cursive in blue,
and write
in my own block letter handwriting
SPANISH 101.

report card

My report card hides in my backpack
for two weeks
a secret I keep from my mother,
terrified to let her see the truth
(because I am more defiant *after* she hits me
than *before*),
until she discovers it, while going through my things
while I sleep, and wakes me
with open-palmed *SLAP SLAP SLAPS*!
screaming, "What is this?!"

I scream back
"Straight A's! I made the honor roll! Most parents would be proud."
Mom is not proud
as the report card is crushed
into my face by the heel of her hand,
blunt force heavy enough
to crush blood from my nose
like pressing corn flour dough balls into a flat tortilla,
screaming, "I told you NOT to take Spanish!!"
Violence brings bravery in me,
wanting desperately to speak the language in my blood,
shouting,
"Te odio. Deha de arruinar mi vida."

Mom, whom I grew inside, the flower from which I was born,
punishes me again and again with her fists, hissing that I am
    wrong,
though never giving me
a reason
why.

maricón

White kids at school call me a "beaner"
Black kids at school call me "white trash"
Kids who eat at the Chinese restaurant where my mom works
    call me "egg drop soup"
Today, a Mexican kid calls me something new: maricón.

It isn't the word that bothers me, but the way he said it. How he
    spat on the ground after.
I try to look it up in my English-Spanish dictionary.
It isn't there.
So in class, I ask the teacher, "*¿Cómo se dice* maricón *en inglés?*"

Half the students laugh.
I guess they already know.
Once again, I'm the dumbest kid in the room.

Someone shouts, "You don't know how to speak your own
    language?"
So I flip him off.

The teacher gives me detention,
even though I wasn't being funny.

I just wanted to know.

confused

I sit across from the principal
slumped back in my too-baggy jeans, my too-big long-sleeved
   shirt,
my arms crossed in a shield under
my I-don't-give-a-shit face
and the principal says, "I don't understand you, Rex.
You're either in my office because you made honor roll
or because you were fighting,
again."
I shrug.
"You have potential," he says,
"you could be going places . . .
if you clean up your act."
I snort. Roll my eyes.
But I am thinking,
What would Abuela say?

The principal says,
"Focus on making good grades.
Stop taking the bait,
stop throwing punches."
He waits for a response.
He doesn't get one.
He asks, "What do you want to be when you grow up?"

I don't say anything,
because a chasm opens up in me,
a future full of darkness,
because I already know:

I won't make it past graduation.

no

When Abuela comes to visit, she asks,
"Do you want to go to the mall? I'll buy you some clothes."
"No."
"Do you want to go to the grocery store? I'll buy you your
    favorite foods."
"No."
"Do you want to go to a comic book store? I'll buy you
    whatever you want to read."
"No!! I don't want to go anywhere, okay?!"

I don't mean to yell. But I don't apologize
even though I know I should.
Her feelings are hurt.

But I don't want to go anywhere where we might bump into
    kids from school.

I love my Abuela. I do.
But she's embarrassing.
She's one more thing
for others to make fun of me with.

And I can't.

I can't do it.

I'm too tired.

another visit

"Your grandmother asked if she could come visit," Mom says.
"Can't we go visit her instead?"
"Why?" Mom asks with a sneer, "I thought you loved her."
"I do. It's just . . . I'd rather go to Abilene . . ."
Arms crossed, Mom looks me up and down . . .
catching me, like a fish in her hook,
she smirks, triumphant,
"You're ashamed of her . . . You little brat. After everything she
    does for you."
"I'm not ashamed!" I'm already shouting,
"I just . . . her clothes, the way she talks—"

SLAP.

For once,
I know
and agree with Mom's hand:

I deserved that.

foil

When I check the mail each day,
it is junk mail
or bills
or overdue bills
or bills with red ink for final notice
or something with the familiar penmanship
of pleasant stick figures.

Before I open the white envelope
addressed to me,
I hear the familiar crinkle of the silver paper inside,
foil
not wrapped around minty gum, but
folded around cash.

Sometimes it is five dollars, sometimes it is ten, or twenty,
sometimes quarters are taped to the page,
her gently spelled English letters saying:

> Spend this on something just for you.
> You deserve it.
> You are special.
> Te amo siempre.
> —G-Ma

education

The next time I see Abuela, she asks for my report card.
She examines it.
"I am very proud of your grades."
"I didn't make straight A's. I made a B– in biology."
"You will do better next time."
"What if I don't?"
"Then you will work harder the time after that."
"But what if I'm not good enough? Maybe I'm not cut out for college.
  Maybe I should give up now, stop wasting my time, stop wasting your
  time."

Abuela grabs my arm, squeezing,
not to punish me, or hurt me, but to grab my attention.
"You are good enough.
You will go to college.
You will not give up. You are not wasting anyone's time by
  trying."
"How do you know?"

"Because I know these things.
Once you have an education?
No one can ever take it away.
Once you have learned something,
that is yours forever."

She gives me the slightest of shakes, then lets go my arm.
I fall into her, hugging her,
wanting to never let go.

junior year schedule

Advanced Placement Art
Advanced Placement English
Advanced Placement Chemistry
Advanced Placement History
Honors Calculus / Honors Geometry
World Literature & Culture / Intro to Psychology
Physical Education

This year,
I tell myself,
I will make straight A's.
I will make straight A's.
I will make straight A's.

                                        And I do.

junior year names

Beaner.
Faggot.
Wetback.
Trailer trash.
Homeless.
Hobo.
Homo.
Nelly.
Pussy.
AIDS patient.
Fudge-packer.
Freak.
Weirdo.
Queer.
Loser.
Worthless.

This year,
I tell myself,
I will not fight.
I will not fight.
I will not fight.

                                        And I don't.

the quiet plan

Abuela calls when Sam and Mom are at work.
Her advice: "Let them say what they want. Do not fight back."
"I don't."
"Do they still . . ."
"Yeah."
"Do you want to come live with me?"
"You know I do."
"ACU has a program called Junior Scholars,
the summer before your senior year of high school,
you will attend college classes, you will live in a dorm, you will
    have a lunch card . . .
Do you want to apply?"
"You know I can't afford it."
"They have scholarships.
With your grades, with your writing, you will get it."
"Mom will never agree to it."
"It is school. She won't argue."
"Wanna bet?"
"I will not bet on your future. Your future will be bright."
"You have more faith than I do."
"God will provide."
"He hasn't so far."
"He has. He gave you me."
" . . ."

I cannot argue with that.

letter

When I check the mail,
there is a letter addressed to me,
from Abilene Christian University.
I don't want to open it.
What if they say no?
I am willing to work hard.
I have worked hard. Harder than anyone I know—
except Abuela.

And I am not a Christian.
I refused to be baptized for a god
that lets children suffer.
I worry
God won't give this to me.
If there is a god.

I take the letter inside. My hands shake.
Mom gets sick of my pacing, snatches it from my grasp.
"Just give it to me. I'll open it."

She opens it.
Her face is written in disappointment.
"I didn't get it, did I?"
"No," she says.
"You did."

hugs

"It's only six weeks," I tell Ford,
who refuses to say good-bye. He will not look at me,
let alone speak to me.
I wrap my arms around him,
burying my quiet tears in his neck,
whispering, *"You have to call me, okay? Or pick up when I call you."*
"No," he says.
"I love you."
"I don't care!"

Four weeks sober,
and trying to make up for the past,
Sam shakes my hand. "Good luck."
"Thanks."

Mom wraps her arms around me, hugging me tight,
the comfort alien.
I wonder if she is hugging me for me,
for her,
or for my aunt, who is watching, who believes my mother still
    has a heart.
Mom says, "I'll miss you."
"Will you?" I ask.
"Of course, silly," she says.
"Now I have to pay a babysitter to watch your brother."

courses

My scholarship covers three courses:
ENG 101—Intro to English Literature (which I chose).
PSY 101—Intro to Psychology (which I chose).
BIB 101—Intro to Bible Studies (which is required).

The Junior Scholars program has thirty-eight students.
Including me, only seven are boys,
the rest are girls.
Half of us go to public school, a few to private,
the rest are homeschooled.
Maybe a third of my peers are the offspring of a preacher or
    pastor.

No one here reminds me of me.
They are too innocent.

prayer circle

Friday night, we meet in the center of the football field,
the darkness punctuated by bright lights
beaming down on just us youth.
Tonight we are going to pray,
for the world, for non-Christians, for our friends and family and
    loved ones,
and discuss how we're feeling
about being away from home,
many of us for the first time.

Everyone takes a turn, as the bible goes from one hand to the
    next,
talking about how they feel God
and Jesus
and the Holy Light
inside them,
filling them with strength,
and confidence,
and hope.

When it is my turn, I cannot speak, my lips quiver, until
I burst into tears,
blubbering,
sobbing,
unable to catch my breath,
even as my fellows surround me with hugs, and love, and
    audible prayers.

After, many of them come to me, and say,
"You were amazing."
"That was beautiful."
"Thank you for sharing."
"I was a mess."

"No. That was god's light shining through you,
making you strong enough to bare your true feelings in front
    of us.
You are a hero.
So brave."

They do not understand that I was crying
because I didn't feel anything at all.
As always . . .

                        I feel scared.
                        I feel broken.
                        I feel damaged.
                        I feel forgotten.
                        I feel alone.

But that night,
sleeping on the floor
of my new friends' dorm room,
I lie awake
watching the moon outside the window
watching me
feeling something new inside the
dark recesses of my soul . . .

                        some dim light
                        shining
                        the
                        tiniest
                        beam
                        of
                        hope.

I am not sure if I believe in God
but I believe in angels,
or at least one angel.
Her name is Abuela.

a new abilene

This is the town where I was born,
where my abuela lives,
where I have returned again and again
like a boomerang,
flung out on the winds of the world, only to return to sender.

But with this summer away
from Mom, from Sam, from the usual,
this place becomes new again.

I discover
coffee shops with poetry readings,
dry lake beds to watch sunsets over
swimming holes with just enough water to splash around,
a dance club that allows minors, drawing large red X's on the
    back of our hands,
and friends, not across the street, but from all over Texas and
    other states.

Yes, there is prayer
(which causes my eyes to roll)
but there is laughter and wine coolers and make-out sessions
    with Bella
(though I'm thinking of Ben)
and a whole existence without screaming, without violence,
    without . . .
(my usual life).

I realize with a week to go
I do not want to go home.

the quiet plan (part two)

On the last day, Abuela picks me up at my dorm.
I will spend the night with her
before Mom comes tomorrow to pick me up.
Abuela asks, "Did you . . ."
"Enjoy it? Yeah. I did."
"Do you want to come live with me?"
"You know I do."
"ACU has another program, called Local Scholars,
if you graduate from a local high school in Abilene,
they will pay for your tuition for four years, sixty-four thousand
    dollars,
your college will be free . . .
Do you want to apply?"
"I won't get it."
"You were a Junior Scholar. You will be a Local Scholar too.
With your grades, with your writing, you will get it."
"Mom will never agree to it."
"It's college. She can't argue."
"She can. She will."
"You are almost an adult. This is your decision. This is your
    future."
"You really think so?"
"God will provide."
"He . . ."
I want to say he hasn't provided,
but in one way,
he has.
"He gave me you."

So I ask,
"How do I apply?"

argument

Mom shouts, "You're not even a Christian!"
"It's a free education!"
"Nothing is free! Everything has a price.
And those people will brainwash you."
"Please. They tried this summer. It didn't work."
"Then why do you want to go back?!"

> Because it is not here.
> Because you are not there.
> Because I can have a life away from you.
> But what I say is,

"'Cause it's sixty-four thousand dollars!"
"It's just money!"
"No, it's an education!"
"In Abilene?!"
"It's not that bad!"
"Why can't you go to community college here?
You can keep living with me, and drive to school. We'll get you
   a car."
"You won't even let me take driver's ed!"
"Fine, I'll let you! If you stay!"
"I need to do this."
"Why?!"

> Because it is not here.
> Because you are not there.
> Because I can have a life away from you.
> But what I say is,

"'Cause I have a real shot at this."
"You won't get it."
"I won't if I don't try."
"Did my mother put you up to this?"
"What? No!"
"Because she's always wanted you to come live with her. She
   thinks I'm an unfit mother."

"That's . . . crazy. You're a . . . great . . . mother," I lie.
"She doesn't think so."
"Who cares what she thinks?"

                         I do.

"You really want to go to ACU?"
"I don't know. Maybe. But I definitely want a free ride.
And if I go to Abilene High, I could get one."
"Let me think about it."
"Okay."
"I only want the best for you," she says.

                         No.
                         You want what's best for you.
                         You always have.
                         I am secondary.

                         Not like Abuela.
                         Abuela puts me first.

5
SENIOR YEAR

my room

"Which room should I take?" I ask.
Abuela laughs. "Any room you want."
I could pick the room between the kitchen and the garage, but
    it's too small.
I could pick the room with the front window, but that is Aunt
    Lora's old room.
I could pick the room that I have always stayed in—
so I do.

I drop my duffle bag and a box of books (and comics) in the
    corner.
It's all I brought. I travel light.
No need to pretend that anything is permanent,
I know better.
Mom has taught me that much.

Right now, in Abuela's house . . . no, in *our* house,
in the guest room, which has become *my* room,
I throw myself on the bed. My head on a foam pillow,
where one foot away (a mere twelve inches
through a wall), Abuela rests her head.

My new room is ten feet by ten feet,
with the familiar rough carpet the color of a skinned knee scab
with wood paneling (that is not real wood)
with a white ceiling (with stars that glow in the dark),
and an empty closet, which Abuela will soon fill with clothes of
    my choosing.

I feel born again,
a life reset at sixteen
a senior in high school
attending driver's ed

ready to be a new student
       at a new school
             with a new life.

backyard (#3)

Jason's house is across South Jackson Drive from Abuela's.
It is one story,
painted green by someone else,
who only parks their truck in the driveway, not in the yard.

I ring the doorbell.
A man answers the door, his stomach pushing at his shirt, a
    beer in hand.
I ask,
"Is Jason here?"
He says,
"No one here by that name."
Adding,
"Last folks who lived here had a kid, a boy I think, 'bout your
    age.
Maybe that was him.
But he's gone now."

I think,
so is the little boy that used to know him.

chauffeur

Abuela takes me to the doctor.
Abuela takes me to the barber.
Abuela takes me to the bookstore.
Abuela takes me to the post office.
Abuela takes me to the grocery store.
Abuela takes me to the comic book store.
Abuela takes me to the video rental store.
Abuela takes me to the shoe store (for new shoes).
Abuela takes me to the book, music, and movie store.
Abuela takes me to the Dyess Air Force Base commissary.
Abuela takes me to the high school to register for my classes.
Abuela takes me to the mall, shopping for clothes (and
    Chick-fil-A).
Abuela takes me to—
*"Abuela, I don't want you driving me everywhere . . . it's too much. I can
    take the bus."*
"No. The bus is not safe. And I will not drive you everywhere.
You will finish driver's education, get your license, and drive
    yourself."
"Abuela, I don't have a car."
"Then we will get you one. You are an adult. You have been for
    a long time.
It is time someone started treating you like it."
"Abuela, a car? That's too much."
"I will only pay for the deposit. You will pay for the rest,
the monthly payment and insurance.
Is that fair?"
"More than fair,"
I say.
And it is.

grape jelly

Before driver's ed class,
Abuela takes me to McDonald's for breakfast.
She lets me order whatever I want
which means I order
pancakes,
scrambled eggs,
hash browns (and extra hash browns), which come in a paper
   sleeve, slick with grease
and an English muffin,
which I will slather in butter
and grape jelly.

Abuela smiles, saying,
"Make that two."

We eat together,
quietly smacking,
while she asks what I need for school.
When we are done,
I take the trays full of Styrofoam plates, crumbled paper
   sleeves, and plastic cutlery,
and throw it all away,
wondering if my sticky crumbs will end up
in a landfill, or the ocean.

Returning to the table, I find Abuela
holding a single serving of grape jelly,
and eating it delicately
with a plastic spoon
as if it were
pudding.

My face flushes with embarrassment,

worried someone might see, make fun, laugh.
I ask, *"What are you doing?"*
"Eating dessert."
"If you're still hungry, order more food. They have actual dessert, you know."
She shakes her head at me.
"Why? This is free."
"Who does that? Who eats jelly for dessert?"
Abuela says,
"I do."

My fear of being seen
evaporates
into thin air,
as Abuela and I laugh
together.

hallway

Each morning,
I wake,
and need to pee.
Groggy,
I stumble from bed,
out of my room,
and past the hamper,
where I used to hide as a boy,
waiting for Abuela to find me.

And each time
I pass it,
I cannot help
but
       smile.

work

At Crystal's Pizza and Spaghetti Warehouse,
I bus tables, carting heavy gray tubs
of red see-through cups, used metal silverware, and khaki
    plastic plates
crusted with crusts of pizza, spaghetti ends, and abandoned
    meatballs
to the back where large sinks wait for me to wash it all before
    stacking on trays
that go through a dishwasher, spraying hot steam in my face
    and on my arms
coming out the other end spotless, as if new, ready to return to
    the kitchen window,
where they will be used again and again,
from 5 p.m. until 11 p.m., at which point
I stock the shelves and the pantry and
put the contents of the salad bar back into the freezer
that fogs my glasses until I cannot see . . .

At midnight, after the dining hall lights have dimmed,
the red neon light switched from "Open, come see us!" to
    "Closed 'til tomorrow! See ya then!"
I walk outside,
smelling of old food and soap, my clothes splashed with
    marinara and ranch dressing,
to find Abuela waiting for me in the driver's seat of her car,
yawning, but happy to see me,
to drive me home
so that I can get six hours of sleep before school tomorrow.

I do not like my job (a busboy)
but in a college town, jobs are hard to come by.
I think of Abuela, when she was my age, in shoes with holes,
walking across the border, Mexico into Texas,

to clean homes for nickels and dimes.
I will do whatever it takes
to save up enough money
for my first month's car payment and insurance,
and make Abuela proud.

rumors

Someone started a rumor that I was kicked out of my last
    school for fighting.
Someone started a rumor that I am gay, or bisexual, or a
    prostitute.
Someone started a rumor that I went to warehouse raves in
    Dallas.
Someone started a rumor that I buy my clothes with drug
    money.
Someone started a rumor that I am some kind of sex addict.
Someone started a rumor that I am some kind of genius.
Someone started a rumor that I am really kind of cool.

I do not care what people say anymore
so I do not correct people when they ask.
Instead, I shrug.
The rumors work to my advantage,
making new friends made easy.
I find myself friendly with the Student Council,
with kids from the Junior Scholars program,
with Christians and non-Christians,
with the Literary Club,
with the theater kids,
with the potheads,
with kids itching to leave Abilene, to go to "the big city,"
where they think me from, even though Grapevine is only a
    suburb of Dallas / Fort Worth.
I am invited to parties,
which I decline because of work,
which makes people want me to come even more.
I do not understand any of my popularity,
except that I am new,
and all kids like to play
with new toys.

paintings

The portrait is of an old mill,
a farmhouse, a cow,
and a red tractor.
The red is so brilliant, so bright,
it breathes life into the drab of
a gray mill
a brown farmhouse
a black and white cow.
The tractor glows, like a beating heart,
filled with life
brighter than the sun behind it.

I have always liked this painting, hanging in Abuela's living
    room,
probably because I imagine
the cow drives the red tractor when no one is watching.

But when I come home after school,
the painting is gone.
"Where's the cow and the red tractor?"

Abuela says, "I returned it to the library."
"I don't understand."
"You can check out framed art from the public library.
When you are done, you take it back, exchange it for something
    new."
"Why borrow artwork? Why not just buy it?"
"Buy art?
When I can have it for free?
When I can exchange it for something else, anytime I want?"
Abuela laughs.
"Don't be silly.
I'd rather spend my money on something that matters,
like you."

car

A Toyota Corolla,
dark gray, with black trim, four doors, sleek
like a rocket,
shot out of space and into my hands
where the keys lie.
I can hardly believe when the salesman says,
"Congratulations on your first car."

I look at Abuela,
who beams, kisses me on the forehead,
and says, "Please, drive carefully."

mirror (but older)

Naked,
seventeen years old,
I stand in front of the guest bathroom counter
to stare at myself, for a long time,
in the mirror hanging over the sink.
trying to see what others see,
see what my new friends seem to like.

What I see is what I have seen for years,
my zits,
my glasses,
my long hair,
my shortness,
my scrawniness,
though there is something different about me too.

I do not see it at first,
even as I stare over every pore,
checking my skin,
too tan in some places, too pale in others . . .

Slowly, I start to realize
I stand taller,
stand firmer,
stand stronger,
emit a new kind of warmth,

As if the stress, the violence, the degradation, the heartache of
    my old home
somehow stunted me,
pushed me down,
crushed me under its weight,
and froze me to the core.

Now though . . .

This.
This is all of me
as taken in by the mirror:
still a striped animal, a human zebra,
but
standing taller,
painted beautiful,
by Abuela's own hand.

consent

I do not enjoy going, but I go,
to church
every Sunday,
with Abuela, or with friends,
because everyone in this town goes.

After,
on the drive home I ask my grandmother,
"Were you always Church of Christ?"
"No," Abuela says,
"growing up, my family was Mormon."
*"Mormon?! How did I not know that? Aren't they the ones with tons of
    wives?"*
"Mormons are wonderful people.
They were all over Mexico,
providing a good value system to all,
though it was very unusual not to be Catholic.
My parents embraced Mormon culture,
and it was good in our lives.
We went to church on Sundays,
and never asked questions,
wearing our poor, but clean, clothes.
Our shoes were so old, we wore them until they fell off,
even as we walked miles and miles to cemeteries to baptize the
    dead."
"You baptized the dead?"
"My parents did.
Everyone deserves a chance to go to heaven."
"What if they aren't Mormon? What if they don't believe?
Baptizing someone without their consent seems wrong."
Abuela's lips tighten
as she takes my hand and squeezes hard, a warning in her eyes,
"Do not judge things you do not understand."

at church (once again)

At church,
for some reason,
I still giggle and snort,
when everyone bows their heads in prayer,
as if I cannot control myself, when everyone is quiet.

Abuela looks at me.
And I bite my tongue,
pinching myself (rather hard)
where my butt cheek meets my thigh
which helps me
shush the memories
of being a little boy
and laughing
freely.

fried

Each week, Abuela gives me fifty dollars, and says,
"Go to H-E-B and buy whatever you want to eat."
My new diet is Eggo waffles, canned SpaghettiOs,
Pop-Tarts, gallons of ice cream,
and crunchy taco shells filled to the brim with ground beef,
    cheese, and salsa
that I make myself.

Today, in the frozen food aisle,
I see a box of popcorn shrimp, like at restaurants.
My stomach grumbles in delight.

At home, I read the directions on how to fry the tiny shrimp.
I pour oil into a pot and turn the burner on.
After half an hour, I am still waiting
for the oil to bubble like water.
I turn the heat to HIGH and put a lid on it
when the phone rings.

Melanie got in a fight with her boyfriend again.
The kitchen phone cord is torn, making static,
so I head to my room to talk there,
consoling my friend until
the house alarm is screaming.

Down the hall, black smoke rolls across the ceiling from a
    kitchen on fire.
On the stove, the pot lid hops boiling to hold in storm clouds
    and spots of dancing flame.
There is no fire extinguisher in sight. I can't recall what to do,
    except no water on oil.
So I grab the pot handle and run outside, onto the back patio,
and throw.

The scorched pot crash-lands, throwing boiled oil back at me
splashing onto my right hand, forearm, elbow, and arm,
like a dozen wasps stinging at once,
burning
as globs of heat cling to my skin and
I scream, trying to pull off the hardening gelatinous drops,
singed tight to my skin like hot glue.
But there's no time to cry
with a fire inside.

Running back to the kitchen, I douse flames with baking
    powder,
using dish towels to smother, pat, slap, pat, slap
until they have every one of them,
all gone out.

The kitchen, once shades of happy yellow and green,
is now dusted white
over scorches of black,
and I worry that Abuela will be done with me.

I pace the house,
sick to my stomach
at what her reaction will be.
I scrub and clean what I can,
but it is no use.

When Abuela comes home,
her teeth grit together,
biting down her fury, at a destroyed kitchen
 . . . though in equal measure,
worried over my burns.
She does not scream. She does not hit.
She ignores me as I apologize again and again and again,
begging her not to send me home to Mom and Sam,

instead, focused on tending
to my wounds.
"You will live," she finally says,
"but my kitchen will need to be replaced."

scars

Sometimes in class, I forget the board and the teacher,
noticing my scars,
old and new
alike.

Claw marks on my arm from Mom.
A cigarette burn on my leg from Sam.
The tear on my knee from a nail in an above-ground pool.
Skid marks up my shins from biking and skateboarding with
    friends.
A knuckle torn from a water bottle thrown.
A line in my hair from stitches after a door swing.
Fresh burns from failing to cook
tiny little shrimp.

And what used to seem upsetting
now tells a story
of my life

and the things I have survived.

confused (again)

I sit across from my principal
sitting up in my too-baggy pants, my too-big plaid button-up,
my arms crossed in a shield under
my new I-kind-of-give-a-shit face
and the principal says, "I don't understand you, Rex.
You're either in my office because you made National Honor
    Society
or because you're mouthing off to teachers . . .
again."
I shrug.
"You have potential," he says,
"you could be going places . . .
If you clean up your act."
I don't snort
But I am thinking,
What will Abuela say?
Why can I not help myself?

The principal says,
"Focus on making good grades.
Stop taking the bait,
stop arguing with everyone."
He waits for a response.
He doesn't get one.
He asks, "Do you want me to call your grandmother?"

And I sit up straighter.
Because the chasm that used to rest inside me
has been filled up,
not completely,
but I'm not so empty anymore.
And now I know:

I might just make it past graduation.

senior year schedule

wake at six in the morning,
sit-ups, push-ups, and breakfast,
homework at seven,
school at eight,
class,
class,
class,
lunch,
class,
class,
class,
class,
home to change, eat, homework,
then to work,
bussing tables, washing dishes, stocking supplies,
then home by midnight
to shower,
then sleep until six.

If Abuela can work eight jobs,
I can do this.

But to be honest,
I always look forward to Saturdays,
when I hang with my friends,
or do nothing at all.

new life

Abilene is easier than Grapevine was.
Both classes and people.
Or maybe, I'm just able to focus for the first time
when a fight does not wait for me at home.

Eighteen-hour days Monday through Friday, school and work.
On weekends, I do
homework with Michelle or get stoned with Carter, or both.

After one semester, I am in the top twenty of my class,
straight A's in all honors and AP classes
(to make Abuela proud),
and I only get detention every other week,
mostly for mouthing off,
and suspended twice,
once for publishing foul language in a school paper, and
once for punching a guy who hit a girl.

For the first time, I am free.
I want to do good all the time,
though I mess up
quite often
(which hurts Abuela, which makes me feel awful).

But I always come home
to Abuela, kissing her on the cheek,
apologizing, and
thanking her for my new life
and promising
to strive
        to be better.

boy interrupted

After school today,
I drive home, singing Cranberries and Smashing Pumpkins,
mouth watering, thinking of Abuela's chicken spaghetti
    leftovers.
I park in the driveway,
and swing the keys around my finger.

I open the front door, make it no more than four steps
into the dark house,
when I am tackled by two shadows,
head slammed into the wall on my way down
"Grab his legs," says one man,
and the other, "Got him!"
Both men over six feet tall,
on top of me, a knee in my neck, another on my spine,
I worry I've been jumped,
that Abuela is being robbed,
before realizing
that I know these voices,
and look up
to see nearby—
Mom.

Sam grabs my hair, knee pressing my neck into the blood-
    colored carpet,
Mom asking, "What are you taking? Speed? Angel dust?
    PCP?"
I can't breathe, let alone answer,
when Abuela cries out, "You're hurting him."

Mom holds Abuela back, saying, "This is for his own good."
"*Wha—talk—bout?*" I choke,
body smashed against the floor

lungs flattened
by four hundred pounds of two adult henchmen
Sam and his friend Barry.

"We know you're on drugs," Mom shouts. "What are you
    injecting?"
White stars wash over my vision,
the sunless room blanketed in snow drift
from lack of oxygen,
and hitting my head.
The adults are all over me,
ripping my sleeves back
checking my veins,
finding nothing.

"Explain this!!" Mom screams, shoving a cigar box at me.
The box isn't mine. It's Jake's. His weed stash.
If he gets busted one more time,
he's off to military school.
So I did him a favor
and kept it in my room.
Stupid. I know.

Drifting out, away from my body, whispering, "'s—just—weed."
Sam and Barry ease off, letting
my lungs sip the air, like iced tea,
til I am choking, coughing, gasping for more.
"This is a glass pipe!" Mom is shouting.
"For—weed," I rasp.
"And this, this is some kind of—of—"
"Pipe—cleaner," my voice scratches, "for cleaning the pipe. From weed
    resin."
"And this?!"
"A grinder."
"So my son is some kind of marijuana expert now?!"

She descends,
a bird of prey
upon her prey,
slapping and slapping and slapping
until Sam pulls her away,
and Barry steps to the side, uncomfortable,
given that he is Sam's weed dealer.

I hold my aching throat, checking it for all its parts,
glaring at Sam, who used to sell me weed,
making me promise to never tell Mom.
I keep my word.
Instead of crying hypocrite,
I only ask Mom,
"What is this really about? You didn't come here for me. I know you. You
want something."

Mom flies at me, hand raised, but Sam catches her.
A banshee screaming, "Catalina called me because she found
    your drugs,
I was worried."

"Worried? So you attack me?!" Now I am screaming too.

"I'm still your mother," she yells, "and no son of mine is going
    to get mixed up in drugs!"
"It's just weed! Everyone in high school smokes weed!"
"You're going to ruin your life!"
"By making friends and having fun?"
"You'll be a high school dropout!"
"My grades are higher than ever!"
"I'm taking your car!"

I stop.
Realizing.

"That's what this is about."

"You need to be punished!" she screams.
"If you want to punish me, take the keys. Let the air out of the tires.
Leave the car in the garage, and take the battery. But leave it here."

"No," Mom says. "That car is mine."
"You have a car."
"It stopped working."
"So you're taking mine."
Then she's screaming, "No teenager should have a *new* car.
Not when I'm driving a piece of shit!"

"See?" I say to the room. *"This isn't about me and drugs. This is*
about her."

Barry looks to the side. Sam looks at Mom. Mom glares at me.
    I look at Abuela.

I rage, shouting, *"What were you thinking, Abuela? Inviting this*
    lunatic into your home.
Into our *home. You should have talked to me first. Why did you call her?*
    Why?!"

Abuela cries. Weak, she sits on the couch.

"Give me the keys," Mom says.
"No," I say.
"Give me the fucking keys, Rex."
"You'll have to pry them out of my cold dead fingers."

Then she's on top of me, pulling my hair, slapping, punching. I
    won't let go.
I won't give them up.
Abuela folds first.

"Stop! Stop hurting him! I have the spare set."
"Don't!" I shout
but too late.

Within five minutes, Barry, Sam, and Mom are gone.
As if they were never here.
Going back to Grapevine.
Along with my car.

I glare at Abuela,
and I can't stop myself from growling,
"This is your fault."

new schedule

Michelle picks me up before school in her car, Big Bertha.
Carter takes me home after school in his Ford Bronco.
I do my homework and eat my 4 p.m. dinner
before Abuela drives me to work in silence.

When my shift is over, she is waiting for me in her car.
She drives me home.

Without a word,
I go to my room,
and slam the door.

cutting back

I cut my hours at work
to three nights a week
now that I don't have a car payment and insurance,

I am a senior in high school
and I plan to enjoy it.
And I do.

I spend days and nights with friends.
Abuela's house, an occasional place to sleep
or do homework
or watch TV.

Though I only spend time in my room
because I cannot look at Abuela
(or the living room)
the same way.

This was my new life,
my new home.
Until I was attacked.

Now it is tainted.

One bad day
brought all the old pain
back
as if it were new.

how to party

I see:
Teens drinking til they puke.
Teens drinking Nyquil when they can't find booze.
Teens smoking cigarettes and rolling dice, gambling for cash.
Teens smoking weed til they can't talk.
Teens rolling up tea leaves and smoking that.
Teens dropping acid.
Teens doing whippits off whipped cream cans.
Teens snorting coke to look cool.

They all seem like children.
I've seen too much to be that stupid.
But
I'm not judging.

(Though I do laugh, when I hide their keys
and don't give them back til they're sober.)

Yes, I drink.
Yes, I smoke weed.
But I am not stupid.

I make some rules for me:
I do not drink and drive.
I do not smoke weed and drive.
I do only a little bit of booze or weed at a time.
I keep a good head on my shoulders.

Because I still
do not want
to fuck up
my second chance.

apologies

"I'm sorry,"
Abuela says.
"I should have talked to you first.
But I was scared."

I say, "*I know.*"
Then, "*I'm sorry too.*"

We do not hug
as I walk into my room
and close the door.

child support

The first Sunday afternoon
of every month
you can find Abuela
sitting at the kitchen table
paying her bills
by writing checks.

I shouldn't, but I look.

"Please tell me you're not still paying for that car," I say.
"Mom took it. It's her responsibility now."
"I have to pay for it," Abuela whispers. "It's in my name.
If I don't, your mom won't pay for it.
She will ruin my credit."
*"So you're making payments on a car for her to drive around in?
In my car?"*
"She says she'll give it back to you."
"When?"
Abuela wipes away tears.

I pick up the phone and call Mom.
*"If you're going to steal my car,
you could at least have the decency to pay for it."*
"It's your car, not mine."
"Then why are you the one driving it around?"
"Because I'm your mother, that's why!"
"Give it back."
"I'll give it back to you when you've learned your lesson."
"And when will that be?"
"When I say."
"You're a real piece of work, you know that?"
"Watch it."
"Or what? You'll drive to Abilene and kick my ass?

Be my guest. Feel free to drive here in my car."
"You're getting too big for your own britches, you know that?"
"Why? 'Cause you can't control me anymore?
Or 'cause I'm not your own personal punching bag?"
"I've had it with you speaking to me like this."
"Or maybe it's 'cause you're not getting child support anymore."

"Rex," Abuela says, putting her hand on mine.

On the other line, Mom asks,
"What are you talking about? I still get your dad's check every
    month.
I cash it and I spend it."
*"Wait—aren't you giving that money to Abuela? She's taking care of me
    now."*
I look at Abuela,
in her eyes
I already see the answer.

"What is wrong with you?"
"The world owes me, Rex. And it's about time it started
    paying."
"When are you going to grow up and stop acting like a petulant child?"
"Fuck you, Rex."

Click.

She hangs up on me.

letter (#2)

When I check the mailbox,
I find a letter from ACU.
It's large, and thick.
I set it on the table and wait for Abuela to come home.

"Is that it?" Abuela asks.
"I don't know."
"Why not? Open it."
"I can't. I don't deserve it.
Not after the way I've treated you."

Abuela sits next to me,
hand on my hand.
"We have both made mistakes.
No one is perfect.
Open it."

I open the envelope.
I have been accepted.
I have been given the scholarship.
A full ride.
A free ride.

Abuela and I both laugh until we cry.
Hugging each other
until
the past
is in
the past.

dad

"I won't be able to make it to your graduation,"
he says,
"short notice . . . work . . . responsibilities . . . your mother . . ."
I understand.
I don't want Mom at my graduation either.
But I want Ford there, and they are a package deal.

"But if you want,"
my father says,
"why don't you come to Alabama for the summer?
Get out of Texas. Maybe take a look at colleges here.
With your grades, you can go anywhere."

I say, *"Maybe,"*
knowing I'll never go.
I am as interested in my father
as I am in Alabama,
meaning,

not at all.

graduation lunch

The big day is here.

In the morning,
Sam, Mom, and Ford arrive
(in my car).
I am glad to see my brother.
Mom hugs me.
I do not hug her back.

Aunt Frannie and Donald come over.
We all go to lunch,
to celebrate me
at a fast-food restaurant.

I do not want to be celebrated,
by my mom or by Sam.
Their being here makes me ache,
nervous,
waiting
for the bad to erupt.

Over burgers and fries,
Frannie asks about my plans
for the future. I say, honestly,
"I don't know. College, and then . . .
maybe I'll be an English teacher."

Abuela takes my hand,
squeezes it.
"You can be whatever you want to be,
if you work hard."

I say, *"Thank you.*
I wouldn't have made it here without you."

Mom clears her throat,
stands,
taps her plastic fork
against her paper cup of diet soda.
"Speaking of the future, I have an announcement."

Worry fills me.

"Ford, Sam, and I are moving to Abilene."

I stand up so fast,
my chair falls over,
plastic clacking against tile.
"What?!"

"I've given it a lot of thought,
and we've missed you. If you're going to school here,
then we should be here too.
So we can be together,
one big happy family."

"We've NEVER been a happy family!"
I'm shouting so loud, strangers are staring.
"Who are you kidding?!"

Mom leaps, nails digging into my cheeks as she squeezes,
    hisses,
"It's not up to you. We're coming."

I grab her hands with mine
yanking them away from my face,
squeezing until her knuckles pop,
and say, *"You are not welcome here. This is my home."*

The first hit comes so fast and so hard,
I don't know I've been hit,

until the ringing in my ear calls me back,
my face laid to rest on the greasy slick of a red and white
    checkered floor.
From here, under the booth, I see
a missing fry, a lost straw, a forgotten ketchup packet . . .

I get up,
shake my head,
taste the blood
on my lip,
pick up my chair,
and sit down,
saying,
"If this is what you call happy,
                         I don't want it."

graduation

After the principal says how proud he is,
after the valedictorian gives her speech,
after we have all walked across the stage,
taking our leather case with the diploma inside,
after we have moved the tassel from right to left,
I find my friends, and we hug, and we laugh, and we tear up,
say our good-byes and see-you-laters,
promising to call and write.

After I have graduated, after it is official,
I find Abuela.
Hugging her, whispering,
"I love you.
Thank you for always believing in me."

"What about me?" Mom asks.

"You? You can go fuck yourself."
Then, in the hallways of the stadium,
surrounded by peers and their families,
taking pictures and smiling,
exchanging gifts and letters and hugs,
I take my stand.
"You have ruined the last seventeen years of my life.
And I promise you,
I promise you with my last breath,
you will NOT ruin the next seventeen."

summer

Seventeen,
done with high school,
and on a plane.

I have friends going to Europe, Australia, New York City,
driving to Yellowstone, Yosemite, Big Bend, California,
enjoying their last days of youth,
before college.

Me?
I am going to Prattville, Alabama,
to stay with my father.

Better the parent you don't know,
than the parent you do.

6
THERE AND BACK AGAIN

guest

1549 Piney Way.
A green lake of grass perfectly mowed
surrounding
a new white house with new white columns and a new white
    garage
and two new trees
since everything here is new.

Sandra, my stepmom, and
Laura, my stepsister,
welcome me with hugs.
When I come inside, I drop my bags on the kitchen floor to hug
    my dad,
still wearing his Air Force uniform,
who says,
"Careful! You'll scuff the floor."

He leads me to a room at the front of the house.
"This is the guest room," my father says,
"where you'll be staying."
He does not say, "This is your room," like Abuela,
welcoming me into her house, her home, and her heart.

In this room,
there is a large wooden armoire,
like in *The Lion, the Witch, and the Wardrobe*
and for a second, I open the door, and pretend I am going to
    climb inside
(as if it were my hamper),
saying, *"Well, okay. Bye! I'm off to Narnia!"*

My dad quickly shuts the door,
growling, "This isn't a toy. It's an antique."

This is not 1214 South Jackson Drive.
Already, I miss Abuela.

work

I have three jobs.

A cashier at Food World
where I make four dollars and seventy-five cents an hour.
A clerk at Blowout Video
where I make five dollars and fifteen cents an hour.
A server at Cracker Barrel,
where I make two dollars and thirteen cents an hour
plus tips.

The tips are never good,
and the humidity is sweltering,
and my dad isn't all that nice to me,

making me wonder if I should have stayed in Texas.

call

"How are you?" Abuela asks.
"I'm okay."
"Is your dad's house nice?"
"I guess."
"Are your stepmom and stepsister nice to you?"
"Nicer than my dad."
"What do you mean?"
"Nothing."
"He is your father. Your only father.
It is good to get to know him.
You will not regret it."
"How are things there?"
Abuela is quiet.
"I bought a house for your mom.
Across the street.
Where Jason used to live."
I am stunned.
"What were you thinking? Mom will ruin your life."
Abuela is quiet.
"It's too close. She's not going to change."
"This is good for her. I can help her with Ford.
Having a home is important."
"Having your sanity is more important,
and I don't want you to lose yours over her."
"I am a grown woman.
I can make my own decisions.
You take care of you.
I will take care of things over here."

I cannot help but worry.
Abuela's heart is too tender,
always trying to care for everybody.

Even my mom.

tom

Tom works in the meat department at Food World.
A twenty-year-old butcher
with the kind smile of a cowboy
and a warm laugh that intoxicates me
when we chat on our smoke breaks behind the dumpster
even though I do not smoke.

We both are saving our meager paychecks of dollars and coins
for our first semesters at college
where he wants to major in history,
and I in English.

Tom invites me over on Friday,
to his parents' basement, where he has his own den,
and we eat pizza and play Nintendo,
his knee rubbing against mine,
making me wonder if
it is accidental, or on purpose.

Hours later,
I am still not sure
         until
            he kisses me.

telling

I have known for a long time
deep down in my heart
that I like girls and boys,
and maybe boys a little more
(or a lot more),
ever since I begged Abuela for my pink Care Bear.

I want to call Abuela, and tell her my truth,
but worry her heart will hurt,
because her god and her church do not like my kind
and send us to hell.

So I tell my stepsister instead.

That was a mistake.

barbecue

The back porch,
smoke wafts up, the scent of meat swelling, sweating
from the grill,
my father taking swig after swig from his beer,
holding the bottle harder than usual,
unable to make eye contact with me.
I ask, *"Are you okay?"*

He says, without looking,
"If you choose to be gay,
You are no longer welcome in my house,
You are not part of this family.
You want that lifestyle?
Go live it somewhere else."

I wonder how he knows.
Later, I will see guilt in Laura's eyes,
when she cries, asking me to forgive her,
and I do.
She isn't the one who made my dad do what he did.

He gives me a choice:

#1.
I can stay and be straight,
see a therapist at my own expense,
attend church twice a week,
date a girl from the church (who he approves of),
never talk to anyone of the "homosexual persuasion" again,
and make the "right" choice,
by being normal.

or

#2.
I can go and be gay.
I will not have a family.
I will never know true love.
I will catch AIDS and get sick and die
                                        alone
and make the "wrong" choice
by choosing to be abnormal.

I have been controlled too long,
by Mom
by violence
by hate
by the closet.
I am done being controlled.

The choice is easy
because I have no choice.

I was born this way.

pride

I pick up the phone to call Abuela
to ask for help.

I have two hundred dollars,
and no home
and no family here in Alabama
not anymore.

I think of Abuela,
in church every Wednesday and Sunday,
Church of Christ, where they do not dance, they do not drink,
    and they are not gay.

I think of Sam,
shrugging, "You're not my son.
Ford is my only responsibility."

I think of Mom,
laughing at me, saying, "You left, you're on your own now."
And of course, the fighting that will return, if I return.

Then I think of me,
asking for help,

and decide

not to.

good-bye alabama

If I'm going to be homeless,
I will be homeless somewhere cool:
New Orleans.

So that's where I'm going.
It can't be that hard to find a job,
to get into a college there.

It will be easy.
I'm like a cat,
I always land on my feet.

three months

what is a cat
that always lands on its feet
to do
when there is no solid ground
to land on?

no home
no family
no friendly faces
except those that want something.

nights are colder
days are hotter
the streets are rougher
than I could have imagined.

the things that happen?

I'm . . .

I'm not ready to talk about it.

                              I don't know if I'll ever be.

bridge

the bridge
where i think of jumping
seems too high.

but isn't that the point?

it's late
night punctuated by drops of light
and i think i can't
anymore
so tired
of
it
all.

but
ultimately

i can't
i can't do it
even though i want to
                    i can't jump.

collect call (pay phone)

I dial zero.
"Operator, can I place a collect call?"
My stomach growls a deep guttural growl,
a wild animal
that has not eaten a true meal in five days.

(Even starving, pride fought me,
allowing only one meal a day
to be recovered from a dumpster
or a trash can
or a paper bag tossed to the ground without care,
as though the last ten French fries have no value.
One man's treasure is another man's feast.
Shoo, flies, shoo!)

"Yes! Yes, I'll accept the charges," she says,
her *yes*'s coming out as *jes*'s,
All my strength fails.
I am crying, sobbing,
snotting all over the public phone.
"Rex is that you? Rex?"
It feels like so long since someone knew my name.
Since someone cared enough to call me by it.

"Can you . . . can you send me twenty dollars?" I ask. *"I'm sorry. I
     just . . . I just want to eat."*
"I have been trying to find you," Abuela says.
"But no one knew where you were."
"I'm in New Orleans," I say. *"I'm alive. I've tried to find work. I've tried
     to . . ."*
I cannot speak. I cannot tell her what's happened.
No three months have ever been longer.

She says, "Shhh. Time to come home."
That word . . . home . . . has lost all meaning.
She says, "I will wire you three hundred dollars.
Find a hotel, take a shower, eat, and sleep.
In the morning, come back to Abilene."
I am quiet.

She says, "Please, mijo."
She says, "Por favor."

And I say, "Gracias."

return

The drive from New Orleans to Abilene is ten hours.
From swamps to oceanside to pastures to hill country.
Turning onto Abuela's street, nothing has changed.
1214 South Jackson Drive sits as it has always sat, as if waiting
   for my return.

Some part of me worries, that returning to the town where I
   was born
means that this will be the town where I will die.
Maybe. But not today.
And not anytime soon.

I ring the doorbell.
The first door opens, then Abuela pushes aside the screen door,
air-conditioning greets me, carrying the scent of powder and
   pine
and memories from a lifetime ago, of the little boy I used to be.

Her eyes survey me, and see me.
My five-eight frame twenty pounds lighter,
dark rings under my eyes from sleepless nights, worried of
   attacks,
and a soul weighted with the memories of a season alone,
doing what I had to
to eat,
to live,
to survive.

When she opens her arms, I am reluctant.
I approach
She embraces me, her soft scent and skin, her black silk blouse
the same she wore to my high school graduation.
I do not trust her, or her hug,

as if I don't know her
until
her lips find my ear, and kiss,
gentle
not enough to pop it,
but enough that her breath whispers,
"You are safe."

Then I crumble into her.
She holds me, and lets me cry
as long as I need
and so
I cry
for the longest time.

Though my body does not yet accept it,
the danger has passed.

catching up

Abuela fills me in:

Sam and Mom fought in the front yard
across the street from Abuela's home, while living in Jason's old
    house.
More often than not,
punching each other, bloody,
for all the neighbors to see
until Sam finally left her.

Mom found a new man,
my age, eighteen,
fresh from prison, tattoos on his face, a gold front tooth,
who promised he would kill Sam, Abuela, and me,
if we ever pissed her off.
Luckily, he left too.
Then Mom disappeared with Ford, god knows where
(in my car).

Mom never paid rent,
the house was in Abuela's name.
Her credit is ruined.

The house across the street, where Jason and I used to play,
is now empty, but yesterday,
someone started painting it yellow,
bright yellow,
like sunshine,
after a terrible storm.

finding me

When Abuela goes to work,
I am left alone
(but not in the way I was alone in New Orleans).

I walk around her house
1214 South Jackson Drive:

Red bricks, white trim, white wood beams, a white tin roof.
White walls in the halls and bedrooms, the living room paneled
    by wood (that *isn't* real wood)
and a stone fireplace with wood beams (that *is* real wood).
The carpet is still deep red maroon, except the kitchen,
laid with tan linoleum (that looks like tiles, but *isn't*).
The kitchen bright yellow, unchanged over the years,
except the stove area, replaced after my fire.
But the countertops are still
green, like the pecan tree leaves outside . . .

The end of her hallway has
four doors for people, and
two much-smaller doors for elves,
opening into an empty space
the size of a laundry basket
or a little boy.
Built into the wall,
the wooden doors, smooth and lush brown,
like a Kit Kat milk chocolate bar,
or Abuela's skin, silky and soft.
Like my skin.

I am eighteen-years-young
still learning my way in this world.
But

opening the bottom door, I climb inside,
squeezing and cramming my adult body
into the darkness,
slowing my breath,
inhaling drywall and fabric softener,
hiding,
waiting for someone to remember (and seek)

me.

If I wait long enough,
I know the top door will lift, and
Abuela's face will appear, warm
haloed by light,
a heavenly angel to scare away the shadows (and nightmares),
and ask, "Hola, hamper. Have you seen my grandson?"

The thought makes me laugh out loud,
until I am crying,
not out of upset,
or anger,
or fear,

but out of joy

because I am

finally

<u>HOME</u>

7

NOW

te amo siempre

Decades have gone by.
But
Abuela and I still speak often.

She does not always remember
the pecan trees
or the geese
or even the hamper,
but
when Abuela and I speak,
she says,
"Te amo."
And I say, *"Te amo siempre."*
And she says, "I love you more."
And I say, *"Impossible."*
And I mean it.